10 STUPID THINGS grown-ups say & do

Moss Mashamaite

redOystor

London | Johannesburg | New York

Copyright © 2018 Moss Mashamaite

First Published by ChatWorld Publishing 2006
Second Publication by RedOystor Books 2018
  an Imprint of RedOystor Media (Pty) Ltd
  with permission from Moss & Moss Publishing

All rights reserved. No part of this publication may be reproduced, stored in a retrieval system, or transmitted in any form or by any means, electronic, mechanical, photocopying, recording, or otherwise, be lent, re-sold, hired-out, or otherwise circulated without express written consent of the author.

Published by RedOystor Books
an imprint of RedOystor Media (Pty) Ltd

visit www.redoystor.com for more information
Or contact us at **www.redoystor.com/contact-us**

www.redoystor.com/TenStupidThingsGrownUps
www.facebook.com/TenStupidThing

Cover Design & Layout by **RedOystor Media (Pty) Ltd**

Printed by **novus print**, a Novus Holdings company

Available on Kindle and other retail outlets

ISBN: 978-0-9947217-2-3 (Print)
  978-0-9947217-3-0 (eBook)

IT'S OFFICIAL THERE IS NO CURE FOR STUPIDITY

Contents

Acknowledgments   i

Dedication   iii

Warning   vii

Wanted! A Cure for Stupidity   1

One: YOU CAN'T TEACH AN OLD DOG NEW TRICKS   **27**

Two: IT'S TOO LATE, I'M TOO OLD   **43**

Three: THE FEAR OF CHANGE   **59**

Four: ABANDONING YOUR TALENTS IN PURSUIT OF MAKING A LIVING   **77**

Five: WHAT ARE PEOPLE GOING TO SAY? **91**

Six: FEARING FAILURE **101**

Seven: ABANDONING THE AMBITIONS OF YOUR YOUTH **119**

Eight: WHEN I DIE **131**

Nine: Blar, Blar, Blar... Write your own **143**

Ten: MIGRATING FROM THE WOMB OF SILENCE **149**

About: Moss Mashamaite **171**

Other Stupid Books **175**

Acknowledgments

I would like to acknowledge the following people for their assistance and encouragement to publish this, the second 'stupid' book.

The Chatworld Publishers staff who are beginning to really share in the enthusiasm behind our clever 'stupid books.' They have put their utmost enthusiasm and effort to promote the work and make sure the whole world feels the same way about them as they do. They work like a team of ants to accomplish sometimes feats that even surprise me.

I must specifically thank Elias Letshoene for the layout, design and valuable suggestions. His faith in what we are trying to create in the world is amazing and his full-bodied support as the man in charge of Chatworld is spurring the organization to greater heights.

Tshegwane Mohapi for fiercely believing in me and marketing whatever I produce like it was all there was. Also for her infectious laughter which puts you on the alert. Her poignancy and 'tell it like it is' attitude leaves no doubt whether you are in the right or Wrong.

To my readers out there who have called my name and encouraged me to bring it on. All the people who have bought and enjoyed the first 'stupid book' and showered me with their enthusiasm. You have encouraged me in a positive way and given me nights without sleep so I could bring on what lies beneath to God, the one I should have started with, for clarifying my path and making me understand that the universe is on purpose.

DEDICATION

To the memory of my mothers Mmamarulela Elizabeth Mashamaite and Dorothy Popo Mashamaite. To my mother, or rather; the woman who became my mother after my mother passed on when I was three years old. I remember that for three good years I knew her as my mother until a relative, a full grown adult called me aside and said, 'She is not your mother.' I said, 'No she is my mommy!' She said, 'No, your mommy is in a grave. She died when you were three.' Detail, stupid detail. I cried for the entire day. In the afternoon when my mother came back home I was still crying. She asked me why I was crying, worried; because my eyes were now swollen. I told her what happened during the day. It was her turn to cry. She wept and I joined her.

How could I not, her weeping just confirmed what I had heard earlier. Then she left in a hurry to confront the person who had burst my bubble. I understand she spurted out some verbal fire to the culprit. Whatever she said, no matter what the volume of the rivers of our collective tears, I got the rudest awakening.

I guess I grew up at the age of five. I guess I've been long qualified to write a book such as this one. That was the result of what a Grown-up said to a little boy. But D.P. as she was fondly known, remained my mother in action if not in name.

My late mother Liz resigned from earth to become my guardian angel while DP became my teacher and mentor. I know I had a guardian angel because no matter how tough my circumstances have been in all my life, I have always somehow triumphed. Hell, pit, pig sty; been there done that, but like an inflated ball sunk in a pool of dirty water, I have always bounced back.

Guardian angels do exist, and I swear; my mom must be chief among them. Hey, on her death bed she made my substitute mom swear that she would afford me the same education that she would give to her own children. Signed the deal and then passed on. Now that woman was a closer. She lived a short life, dying in her thirties. She made sure she gave birth to me before her short life came to an end and signed a contract which would ensure I could accomplish what I came here for. She was both my mother and agent.

I spent the first two years and a couple of months in the hospital. I was a hospital baby raised by nurses; loved greatly by a woman who knew her time was short. As soon as I became aware that my mom's last mission was me; which she accomplished even though her body was Weak. I decided I would make her proud letting her know it was all worthwhile. Dying, she was still commanding authority and signing deals. "

Then there was D.P. my substitute mother. Awesome in all respects. I watched her throughout her life, unfolding into one great being after another; reincarnating into higher forms until she was snapped into higher service. I think my cousins only discovered she was a great woman when she passed on. I knew it from day one.

She never stopped learning; she never stopped growing; she never stopped climbing to the summits of this hill I call Life-On-Earth of which I personally yearn to be king, if only to make her proud that through me, she contributed.

I like to dedicate my books to the women in my life. Of course I love women and I have had special ones. What would a man be without a woman or women?

When James Brown sang, 'This is a man's world!' He was probably high on weed, his mother should have slapped his face really hard.

How can somebody who survived on the nipple, and grew up on a breast diet, say something stupid like that. One of the ten stupid things James Brown ever said must be 'This is-a man's World'. He even repeated the Words.

This book is dedicated to the two real Grown-ups I have ever known; my mother Liz and my aunt DP.

WARNING

This book is rated PG. Parental guidance is advised.
Before you read each chapter call your parents and tell them what you are about to read. Ask them to guide you. When they have thoroughly guided you, read.
After you have read call your parents again. This time irate. Ask them Why they never told you all these things before. After you finish reading this book, call your college or university principal and ask for a discount on your education. Ask him/her why they did not include a course on marriage and being a married woman when this was such an important eventuality in your life. If he/she refuses with a discount call me. Since at this time your airtime would be depleted, send me a please call me.

"The older I grow the more I distrust the familiar doctrine that age brings wisdom."
 - *H L Mencken*

Wanted:

A Cure for Stupidity

If there is one thing you must know about age is that it doesn't guarantee that you have grown. Not my words, but feel free to do with them as you see fit.

I surfed the Internet, scoured through the Encyclopaedia Britannica, even ransacked the dusty pages of the Bible; I plunged into the Al Quran and fumbled through the Bhagavad-Gita. I peered into the Wisdom of Solomon and Confucius and I was left solemn and confused. I called friends and relatives, acquaintances and enemies. I consulted with doctors, pharmacists and alchemists, even politicians and robbers. I inquired of prophets and idiots, even certified lunatics.

In search of what? A cure! A cure for stupidity.

I got no joy out of my quest. I called a committee and summoned a tribunal, I invited a '*lekgotla*' and nobody pitched. Then I decided it's official, there is no cure for stupidity!

Stupid is a hectic English word. It is not complimentary and therefore I have my fears. But then again this is not a complimentary session - it is rather a war of words.

I have declared war on stupidity and I have in my arsenal the most lethal force in the universe trained against it.

The written word.

If any stray word hits you, do not take it personally; consider yourself caught in the crossfire.

So in the course of executing this war against stupidity, I am going to be seen hurling insults at the most enfranchised members of any society, the Grown-ups.

Risky? Yes!

Stupid? Maybe.

Necessary? Absolutely!

My fear though is that these are the people who have memorized the words, 'Don't talk to me talk to my lawyer.'

If after reading this book you want to sue me please give me a courtesy call. I know a very good lawyer that I recommend for such cases. He is my brother-in-law. He works for a great Jewish legal firm. They certainly know how to bill. They charge per second but they are absolutely fantastic. For your comfort they win all their cases because either way they get the cash.

Grown-ups are cool...

I like Grown-ups, I've always liked Grown-ups.

As a child I had uncles and aunts, and grandpas and grandmas.

I also had neighbours I called uncle, aunt, grand-pa and grand-ma.

They were cool too because when I was little they greeted me softly and warmly, sometimes as though I was retarded. They would give me sweets and biscuits, all the seriously delicious stuff when I was little. So how could I not like them?

As I grew up I slowly began to realise how not so cool this group of beings were.

Like everybody else, I grew up being admonished to respect Grown-ups. I asked why?

Innocent question. The only reason I was given was, 'Because they are older.' So respect them because they have more hours on the clock of life than you. It's like respect is been administered on a first come first serve basis.

Wouldn't it be greater to be respected by the younger generation for a reason more respectable than that?

Reminds me of a story I heard:

A little boy asked his father, "Dad, what are ancestors?"

"Well, my boy, I'm one of your ancestors. Your grandfather is another."

The little one had a look of bafflement as if he didn't get it and then abruptly he asked, "Then, why do people brag about them"

The big questions from the little boy were, "Why do people brag about them?"

Why should young people who know you brag about it?

I think Grown-ups should make an effort to earn the respect of the younger generation. Sad thing is I don't think most of us are making any effort at all, and that ticks me off.

How does the younger generation look up to people who are not up there? We are the natural role models for the younger generation in everything we do.

Mundane stuff and serious stuff that involves not just what we do but who we are. We've taught the toddlers to stand up and walk just by their own observation.

We should teach them to do so in ways that are more profound and deeper than baby steps. It is our duty above all else.

...But then again, I hate Grown-ups

Allow me to say this on second thoughts - please?

'I hate Grown-ups!'

I am at the introductory stage of this book so I should be careful, right? This book is made up of paper and I know people do weird things with paper they don't like. For instance old newspapers are used to smoke weed and tobacco.

Some people go to the smallest room in their house with the newspaper, read the sports and the gossip section and then when they come back from the small room they don't have the newspaper anymore. If you go back to the smallest room to check the paper, it is no longer there.

That is perhaps the utmost disrespect I've witnessed. But then again. I have also seen a young man grooming a beard that would make Billy goats envious, simply trying to look like *'the man'*.

I told him with a beard like that, Americans could confuse him for an infamous member of the Taliban and burn him at the stake on national TV, just to make the world finally know that the so-called greatest nation on earth, has succeeded at tracking down the one man that has terrorized the western word for many decades and they brought him to book.

I met him the next day and he was shaved like a Mahatma.

I think he will make a great Grown-up one day.

From an Osama bin whoever-that-is, to Mohandas Gandhi is a hundred and eighty degree turn-around. Anybody who could do that can do anything. That my friend is what I call, great Grown-up tendencies.

Some people wait until their beard is grey and long and their gait strugglish before they decide they are now Grown-ups.

Nobody is going to come to you and tell you, now you are a Grown-up. If you are waiting for an announcement on the PA system at the Jan Tambo - O.R. Smuts Airport in Johannesburg, you are going to wait forever.

My take is, the sooner you make up your mind the better.

I knew a forty year old man who was so excited about a very sporty car, I was twenty seven then, 'Imagine us in that car,' he said.

I can hear people say, 'How have these two young boys made it behind the wheel of that cute thing.

Wow!' He exclaimed.

I looked at him and wondered whether he was doing simple mathematics. Forty plus twenty seven divide by two would be thirty-three and a half. Arithmetically speaking, the two of us made two young dudes.

The forgotten People

Let's further agree that if there is one thing on God's green earth - I hope the Sahara doesn't feel threatened or hurt by this statement - called Grown-up then there must be a thing also called grown—down.

Do we mince our words?

Are we often guilty of calling our grown-downs Grown-ups?

Perhaps.

We invest a lot of time and money on the empowerment and support of young people. We worry about them, write books about them and I am guilty of that – the guiltiest actually.

We hold symposiums about them, sometimes to the exclusion of other members of human society. In our exclusive attention to the young ones we leave out a very important social group — the Grown-ups. A very needy sector of human society I must say.

Contrary to known facts, this group is among the most under-achieving in human society. They are the most *un-creative, un-daring* and *un-energetic* of us all.

Grown-ups have resigned themselves to being the early retirees of modern society, the custodians of the status quo, and proprietors of passion-less lives.

The group that knows everything that does not work yet knows nothing about what works.

They live such routine lives clockwork is varied. They go to work on Monday, Tuesday to Friday. Saturday they attend a funeral. They know enough people to sustain three hundred and sixty five funerals a year. And if the funerals aren't enough, there is an occasional wedding - which they will call wedding of the year when they talk to the bride and groom - or the unveiling of a tombstone to augment the routine.

Sunday they go to church where they are a regular member or an elder. Usually they don't hear the pastor anymore in church because he is either too draining and repetitive, or they simply just don't give a damn.

Ten years later their hair begins to grey.

Ten years later a shinier face located on top of the original is added to their wrinkling original. One year later they retire.

Then they go on a serious Viagra diet, if they can afford it.

According to a survey I saw on Carte Blanche, only 4% of South Africans can look after themselves after retirement. So forget being able to afford Viagra, which is rather expensive. So I've heard.

A couple of years later their head is all face, the only thing that has survived the cleansing ceremony are the ears, which have now become decorative jug handles that don't hear squat.

Soon it's their funeral.

Usually well attended, a result of all the Saturdays they had invested in other people's funerals. If their funeral is well attended they are deemed to have lived great lives.

If a man of vast learning with more degrees that a thermometer or a white man (black man if they are white) or famous politician attends their funeral, that becomes the final endorsement of greatness in the collective eye of their mediocre community.

Who are they really kidding?

Definitely not me.

Question is, "Who is really qualified to be called Grown-ups?"

Let's start with the non-qualifiers going up.

What is Grown-up really?

Most people think they are Grown-up base the count of years they have recoded their presence on earth.

I ask, yet again. What is a Grown-up really?

Is it a person with hair in all the wrong places?

Or is it a person who is in constant loss of hair.

Is it measured in years, figures on a dial or when one inherits more face than head from the ecosystem of the body, or the blooming of the garden on your head? Because you know, some people just let the years slide and then call themselves Grown-ups.

I must clearly state and even argue that 'around' is not such a great trip. Just because you have been 'around' for a while, even around the legendary block, that does not necessarily mean you are Grown-up. But for the purposes of this book, let us decide that Grown-ups are people who have passed youth by their own decision.

Obviously you will have to agree that there is no actual age for that because people decide individually on such matters. In this book I will tackle without much category, ten challenges that all Grown-ups have to face in life that they usually do not handle too well, hence the ten stupid things.

Ten things, the mastery of which would transform any person of any state into higher states of being. I can guarantee this, if you get stuck in and begin to exorcise these demons, if we may dub them so, it is not too late for you to transform yourself and begin a greater life, a life that will leave behind a track for one and sundry to follow.

These challenges include career changes, ridding yourself of the fear of failure and the fear of other people, resuscitating the ambitions of your youth, learning new ways of doing things - as in new technologies.

Having to start afresh in marriage as in divorce and re-marriage that is if you absolutely have to, parenting and how to guide your children into becoming greater people. For that is all parents should aspire to. It is a tragedy to outdo your kids. If that happens your seed degenerates and even if your memory remains on earth, it only remains in the family album.

The truly great can never be buried in a grave. They are just too large for a six foot hole. They are the ones who would in the words of the Apostle Paul say to death, 'Where is your sting?'

They survive death and they survive the grave.

Shakespeare was buried almost four hundred years ago in 1616, but he is still here with us like never before. I don't know about other countries but in the entire English speaking world, you do not pass matric - grade 12 - without studying Shakespeare.

He remains one of the most quoted people who ever lived.

I heard someone say that Hamlet's soliloquy comprises of the most quoted words in the English language, "To be or not to be? That is the question." Just that part but the rest is just as profound.

"Whether 'tis nobler in the mind to suffer the slings and arrows of outrageous fortune, or to take arms against a sea of troubles, and by opposing them, end them? Etcetera, etcetera.

Shakespeare looks down from heaven and proudly utters the Apostle's eternal words, 'Death, where is thy sting?'

Grown-up does not mean not growing anymore because that equals decay.

Grown-up should mean an age of accumulated wisdom, even wealth, especially wealth. It should mean no more excuses for folly, earned respect; an uncanny combination of patience and impatience.

Impatience because your time is fleeting; patience because you have learned about the mills of God that might grind exceedingly slow yet do so exceedingly fine.

Another conversation I overheard also from a little one talking to a much older person. A five year old.

He asks his grandfather: "Grandpa are you still growing?"

"Why do you ask, child?" Inquired the *ou toppie*.

"Well, the top of your head's coming through your hair!"

My contention today is that if the top of your head is not coming through your hair, you are not a Grown-up - you just look so. You've just seen too many summers and winters you are neither hot nor cold - just some lukewarm stupid.

Does this offend you?

I am sorry but somebody's gotta say it like it is and there aren't many people who would love you enough to do that.

I am writing this book not to offend you but to awaken you to a harsh reality before it's too late? I have heard and seen lots of stupid things in my life.

Stupid things like…

I have seen some building entrances adorned with plain outright stupid signs.

'No Dogs And Hawkers Allowed!'

I said to myself, 'Are hawkers now joining the animal kingdom? Is it that bad? Huh?' 'It started as capitalism with the 'haves' and the 'have-nots', now it's the 'haves' and the 'must-nevers?'

Wisdom is, the same hawker you don't allow during the day, if disallowed everywhere, might come back at night with no intention to sell.

VIP Entrance. What are you saying to the rest of us? You are tempting me to tell all my friends, the masses that make this whole event possible to go home because of that insulting stupid sign, and then we can find out who are the real VIP's.

The term VIP is simply insulting, and I am not saying this because I don't think I qualify for the status. In a couple of important occasions, including a great toddler's birthday party - and did she toddle! - I qualified for the insulting letters. It's just that I don't know how anybody could go through this sojourn that is called life thinking of themselves in lesser terms.

I think in the maternity ward all babies born should be pinned with tags like Moss Mashamaite VIP, or Bonolo Lehoko VIP, or Nelson Mandela VIP.

I guess when Rolihlahla was born he didn't look awesome at all; with those small eyes you simply couldn't tell whether he was awake or asleep. That he could become the first democratic President of South Africa, an African titan and a world statesman towering with the likes of Moses of the Pentateuch, Julius Caesar; Jesus Christ, Marcus Aurelius, Martin Luther King, Mahatma Gandhi and King David, was obscured even from the keenest of eyes.

I know some stupid person is going to think this is sacrilegious. How can you compare Nelson Mandela with Jesus Christ? Let me tell you something that is not included in the cost of this book. This is free of charge with a discount!

Jesus has been waiting for people like Nelson Mandela to show up and pitch up to his standard for a very long time. In his own words he said — "... greater works than these shall they do because I go to the father."

Now shut up and continue to read.

So VIP Entrance? Plain outright stupid! And the security guards who watch that entrance - they should go home and snore until it snows in Lagos.

Stupid things are everywhere. I had a bout of flu and consulted with a doctor. He told me to drink a lot of liquids. I said to him, 'Are you insinuating that I caught the flu because I was drinking a lot of solids?'

Then you go to a garage and they are spring cleaning in winter and the sign reads, Slippery When Wet. You ask yourself, who are they telling? Don't we all know. What happened to plain old Slippery?

I saw a big man, a huge brother jogging up the slope and I asked him why. He said with annoyed emphasis, 'To kill the calories!' I know in Shakespeare's Romeo and Juliet, The Montagues wanted to kill the Capulets and the Capulets wanted to kill the Montagues, but the Calories? Everybody is out to kill the calories, and Shakespeare has got nothing to do with this one.

While this brother was jogging, he was also munching on a hot dog. I said but you are munching on a hot dog, what's the point? 'You need to taste this dog, man, it's off the hook.'

He spoke with one side of his cheek bulging.

I said, 'Let me taste it then.' He ran from me like a real athlete and I thought if they could plant a couple of hot dogs on the jogging path, they could kill more of the calories than they ever dreamed possible.

I visited a cousin of mine and she was sick with flu. I went to fetch the medicine that was prescribed for her. It was still sealed and therefore I opened the boxes to administer it to her. I pulled out the leaflet from one of the boxes which read, 'One three times a day'. She said, "Give me one". I said, "Not before we read the fine print". She said it was not necessary it's just off-the-shelf flu medicine. I insisted we read the flyer on the inside of the box.

I began to read:

Side Effects and Special Precautions

Fear, anxiety, confusion and psychotic states (madness in English)

The rise in blood pressure may cause cerebral hemorrhage (bleeding of the brain) anginal pain, palpitation and cardiac arrest (heart attack), Hypo-tension with dizziness and fainting and blushing may occur.

I said to her, "*Cuz*, you only have flu, why would you risk insanity and heart attack and death to get rid of the common cold?"

And you say Witchdoctors are dangerous?

My question is *which doctors* are dangerous?

Maybe the lunatic next door took flu medicine and then ate an orange from a colleague. After reading the side-effects of that flu medicine which one do you think made him crazy? The orange from a colleague or the flu medicine?

Stupid things are everywhere.

What I can't tolerate is stupid people. Young stupid people annoy me. Old ones just straight outright piss me off.

I am writing this book very pissed off, and if you don't read it to the end I am going to be pissed off even worse and you don't want that.

There is a Sotho saying that goes, '*Botlaela bo phalwa ke bogafi*'.

It means it is better to be a lunatic than to be a stupid. Why? Lunacy or psychosis can be cured. And if you can't be cured at least you can be institutionalized.

Weskoppies can take care of that.

As for stupidity . . . there is no cure.

GROWN DOWN SYNDROME (GDS)

I am decidedly not a religious person, but I have no choice in becoming spiritual because man is essentially a spirit.

To deny our spirituality would mean we would resign ourselves to becoming mammals. Which is defined by the Oxford dictionary as, "Warm blooded vertebrates characterized by secretion of milk to feed their young." I do not think that anybody would want to be remembered that way when your number comes up.

Imagine the epitaph:

Here lies Maria Sithole
She was a great vertebrate
A warm blooded mammal
She secreted Grade-A milk for her young ones
And fed them sumptuously on a strict lactose diet, She died at the age of forty nine of milkitis — the infection of the milk

It sounds trivial, but how many graves could become a perfect match for such an epitaph? Plenty if you shift a couple of letters around. To be Grown-up means you have had more than sufficient years in your life to do better than Maria Sithole.

Reflecting upon my business life, I realise that most people I have ever fired were either grown-downs or people who suffered from Grown Down Syndrome (GDS).

I fired a guy who when asked to do something but said it couldn't be done. I wanted him to make a graphic design depicting a man in a bottle. He said it was impossible.

I said to him, "I don't worship at that temple".

He said the only way to get that done would be to find a human sized bottle and put a man inside and photograph him. I told him if we could do that then we wouldn't need a graphic designer, just a camera, a huge bottle and a stupid man.

He said I was being impossible.

I called his line manager and told him to tell the man to go home, permanently. In my companies the 'I-Word' is just as bad and offensive as the 'F-Word,' perhaps slightly worse.

He was dismissed with immediate effect.

He threatened to take me to the CCMA and he did. I went to the CCMA but he was late himself and the guy at the CCMA was just too drunk for his and the CCMA's own good. He came to his own office, looked at me with bloodshot eyes for what seemed like a decade, staggered out of the office and disappeared for what seemed like another decade. After what seemed like two decades later I felt disrespected and was tired of waiting for Mr Impossible and Mr Drunkie Babbalaas.

I went out, got into my car and rushed to attend to more serious people and business. True drama! I can swear by the CCMA and a couple of empty bottles of alcohol.

The next lady I fired also said a similar thing on a very important project she was supposed to run. The thinking that what I wanted done was impossible is the one thing that got her off her job.

She fired herself - basically.

If you say the task cannot be done you are saying you can't get it done, then we ask somebody to do the job who believes it can be done. In other words we replace you with a person with the right thinking, and skills.

So this good lady was not really fired.

She was replaced by somebody who could do the job. She was a grown-down and the sign at the door was very clear. 'Hawkers and Grown-Downs not allowed.

Sorry about the hawkers part, I didn't design the sign, my graphic designer did.

'Young people might have their unique handicaps but they usually don't suffer from such idiosyncrasies as spelled above. They say things like, 'let's give it a shot'. They are not afraid of failure, for to be afraid of failure is to be afraid of success, because it's simply the other side of the same coin.

WHO QUALIFIES TO BE A GROWN-UP?

Firstly it's people who take themselves seriously. People who regard themselves in entrepreneurial terms and run their lives like a business with an annual report at the end of every year. People who have strategic planning sessions with themselves instead of making stupid New Year resolutions.

People who regard themselves as brands.

People who raise their kids to fill leadership roles in all spheres of life. People who continue to learn on a daily basis and improve their knowledge continually. People who set standards for themselves, higher standards beneath which they refuse to conduct their lives.

Non-conformists who follow their hearts and do not give a damn what the babbling masses say.

People who know that life is like a stage, like the great Shakespeare said, we enter and we exit, and they know that within that allotted undeterminable period they've got to do their do's, and that if they don't, there is no extension or redemption for that matter.

Real Grown-ups know they appeared on earth urgently to fulfill an urgent mission. They know that they are a mystery waiting to be revealed, a miracle waiting to happen, and that time is running out and that they don't have forever in this incarnation. They know they are a thing of beauty, a creation of a gazillion coincidences and that their being here alone, is a testimony to the fact that they are special beings with special assignments.

There is a very thin line between psychology and psychosis, just like there is a thin line between genius and insanity, so allow me to bring in at this point in time two very famous psychologists to wrestle it out in my intellectual boxing arena.

In his book, "Modern Man in Search of a Soul," Carl Jung provides some great insights into the developmental stages of adulthood.

Carl Jung was a younger contemporary, even one-time friend of Sigmund Freud. Both were men of passion, and in my opinion on the opposite ends of the evolution of the discipline of psychology.

They separated ideologically and even as friends because they went out seeking different passions. Jung went out looking for the soul (higher states of being) while Freud peeled away because he was fixated on the body (terrestrial states of being). Jung's disagreement with Freud started over the latter's emphasis on sexuality alone as the dominant factor in unconscious motivation.

"Every form of addiction is bad," Jung later said, "no matter whether the narcotic be alcohol or morphine or idealism".

They both contributed greatly to the body of knowledge on the psyche of the homosapien, but I will argue that they came at different levels.

Carl Jung wrestled with higher levels of being.

He believed that an awareness of a higher self is an integral part in the developmental stage of a human Grown-up.

Writing in, "Modern Man in Search of a Soul," he differentiates between four levels or stages of adult development, namely - The Athlete, The Warrior, The States-Person and The Spirit.

When you come to the end of this book you will realise that the ten stupid things happen routinely at the lower levels of adult development than at higher levels.

Stage One- The Athlete

This is the primary time in our adult life where our basic identification with ourselves is physical. At this stage the adult measures their happiness, achievement, even our success by the shape and abilities of our physical body.

Our muscles, our speed, our strength and our beauty; even the lack of all those define the athletic adult.

High or low self-esteem are defined on this basis.

Pretty, firm, gorgeous, strong, lithe, lethal and stunning are the words used to describe success, excellence and achievement.

Ugly, fat, shapeless, (as if any object could ever be shape-less) are associated with failure. A single zit on the face of the athletic adult can ruin their entire week.

People who are role models of adults at this stage of development would be celebrities like, Halle Berry, The Rock, Mandoza, David Beckham, Tyra Banks, Makhaya Ntini, Lucas Radebe, Muhammad Ali, Tiger Woods and Brad Pitt. And this not for what they have achieved but for how they look and are perceived to have achieved or how they are celebrated.

The people mentioned here might themselves be at higher states of being, but to most they represent this level of the athlete.

At this stage life is impossible without a mirror. Performance, attractiveness and achievements are the hallmark of the athlete-adult. The athlete is fixated on the body.

It is important to make it clear, that it is essential to take care of your body and health and looks at any stage of development. That is not negotiable. Looking good is good for you considering that ninety seven percent of earthlings only experience you through their five senses.

While it is good to make it a point you look good, it is another to have your body as the point of your primary identification.

The athlete-adult is a body with a soul other than a spirit being having a bodily experience.

It is important to notice physical beings have physical limitations.

The athlete's success and abilities are limited to what he or she can do physically.

So we must admit that the athlete is a baby adult.

If an accident or an event of nature renders this Grown-up unable to pitch at his/her usual level of being, he/she is ruined.

Some people move in and out of this stage, others transcend it, but there are those who get stuck at this stage for the rest of their lives.

Stage Two - The Warrior

The warrior is nothing but the improved athlete.

The warrior is mostly all ego, separate from all in his own perception and he feels that his mission is to conquer the world so he can declare his superiority.

In the moving film Muhammad Ali, with Will Smith, the chant - 'The Champ is here!' was nothing but a warrior's mantra.

The warrior is self-important and he must accumulate trophies, titles and awards and lots of material objects which he will be quick to show off.

He is simply beyond personal physical prowess, he wants to prove it by outdoing somebody else. He is taking on the world and he goes around with mottoes like, 'The greatest revenge is massive success,' 'I wish my enemies long life so they can see my success'.

The warrior's success must be seen and declared.

He wants to show his superiority and he reckons himself separate from everything and everyone else. He is an individualist who considers himself alone in a world he must beat. Examples of the warrior would be Muhammad Ali, Alexander The Great, Shaka Zulu or Joan of Arc.

Most people who have uttered the words, 'There is no God', no matter how famous, were going through this stage of development.

In their taking on the world they end up trying to take on its creator too. It is not foolishness to declare 'There is no God', it is childishness.

In the warrior stage, status and position in life are dark obsessions.

Call a guy with a PhD, mister instead of doctor and you will know whether he is at the warrior stage or higher. The warrior will correct you vehemently, while somebody at a much advanced stage will take no offence, titles having lost importance in their lives.

I don't mean to judge anybody by all these, what is important to me is to help you locate yourself and begin to move on to the next level.

Remember you can only start from where you are.

While the athlete stage of adulthood is the infant stage, the warrior stage is like the adolescent stage of adulthood.

Sigmund Freud and Carl Jung differed in opinion over the stages of human consciousness because Freud's view of man ended right here — at the warrior stage. Sigmund Freud's man is an athlete and at best a warrior.

As Peter Gay aptly put it, "He opened a window on the unconscious — where, he said, lust, rage and repression battle for supremacy..."

Carl Jung believed that the adult human was capable to grow to higher states than the athlete and the warrior.

Stage Three- The States-Person

At this stage the ego has been subdued and its paranoia with being separate has been dealt with. In other words, we are beginning to understand and believe that we belong to a society bigger than ourselves and that we are not only an integral part of that but that we are that.

Here the adult reaches adulthood as an adult.

The States-Person is concerned with what is important to the other person. He might still be athletic and even a warrior, but he has an inner drive to serve others.

The desire to compare yourself with others falls off.

At this stage you want to be happy and make happy and you are happier when you make happy.

To become most powerful or most attractive gives into lifting someone else to those places. This is close enough to the highest state. Most people we call great are states-persons.

The greatest politicians are mostly states-persons and they hardly transcend to the next stage because of the athlete and warrior dominations in their lives.

This Grown-up does not desire to be more powerful or attractive, all he needs is to be able to contribute and make this world a better place. This is the realm of peace where you are looking at being good to others.

In my opinion and understanding of heaven, the states-person will make it to heaven and there still become an important soul.

When God has a meeting with the gods, the states-person is invited. While the states-person makes it to my heaven, the person at the next state of being does not just make it to heaven, he is heaven personified.

Stage Four- The Spirit

When one enters this stage of life, one begins to understand that there is really something bigger out there. This stage is the realm of the highest self. It is beyond adulthood. It is the state where man begins to understand that he is indeed an extra-terrestrial being deployed here to fulfill a heroic mission.

He is not limited even to his own body.

He becomes a god.

About twenty years ago the charismatic preachers mostly from the U.S. seemed to be on the verge of a revelation. They taught us, 'You are a spirit, you live in a body and you have a soul.' They stopped right there and went no further.

Basically, they gave us spiritual foreplay and left us out in the cold.

None had the guts to explore deeper what that statement really meant, because perhaps they feared to tread deeper into spiritual territories lest they found themselves in the devil's house. Anybody who ventured beyond the common phrase was called new age.

I want to illustrate the fact that you are a spirit, renting a body that you often dote too much on, forgetting that it is simply your temporary caravan.

In 2005 I had what I believe was an out of body experience that left me puzzled for a good number of days. I woke up at night totally perplexed and confused.

I shared the perplexity and confusion with people close to me and I realised that I still hadn't grappled with the meaning of what I had experienced, so I wrote a poem about it, if only to help me understand what happened. It goes:

I FOUND MYSELF

I woke up deep into the night and I wondered where I were
I got out of bed worried that I could not recollect where I was
I went through my house room by room searching, I found nothing
I went downstairs to make sure that perhaps
I did not fall asleep watching a movie
I was not there downstairs
I quit in despair and went back to my bed
Excessively worried that] could not find myself
I entered my bedroom the hunt for me given up
But behold right there I found myself peacefully asleep
I breathed a sigh of relief and I joined myself in delightful sleep
I had found myself

Now the person writing this book, a guy they call Moss Mashamaite is less than 1 of who I am. More than 99% of who I am is invisible. This is just the tip of the iceberg.

This is true of every human being.

The difference with everybody else is that the Grown-up at this stage of development knows this fact personally and experientially.

The reason we have become so ineffectual as compared with God's expectation of us is because we have concentrated on, educated, fed, dressed and worshiped the 1% and left the 99% out in the cold.

Our education systems and our religions zoned in on the l% and retired there. That is why most of religion is about attire, mannerisms, laws and stupid opinions of stupid men.

Imagine what would happen if we could zone in on the rest of us. It was Prof. William James of Harvard University who said, 'We use only 10% of our mental capacity'. And he was talking about something bigger than the mind.

God is a creator — therefore the most spiritual people on earth are not those who are full of goose bumps we call spirits, but those who are able to emulate the creative attribute in God. That is people who know how to manifest their desires. There is no greater religion than that.

Let me extrapolate the 99 — 1% percent equation of human existence further. Let's give, as an example, a man like Mr Kaizer Motaung. If you meet Kaizer today you will see 1% of him. I am not classifying the man according to the four stages here, I am just picking him as an example because most people would know who he is.

Leave Mr. Motaung on a Saturday and go to FNB stadium during a soccer game or just walk around Naturena or go to any city in South Africa or Africa or even England for that matter, you will meet the other 99% of him. He is everywhere.

I have not met Kaizer Motaung many times in my life, but I do not remember one day in my life going to sleep without meeting the other 99% of him, the brand he has created. When the 1% of people like that pass on to the other side, the invisible 99% of them remain and it might never die, forever and ever. These are the Shakespeares', the John Wesleys', the Siddhartha Guatamas', the Ray McCauleys' and the Nelson Mandelas of this world.

At the beginning of the 20th century, a newspaper reporter named Napoleon Hill met one of the geniuses who had been guided to achieve success, Andrew Carnegie, a steel magnate who had become the wealthiest person in the world at that time.

Carnegie advised Hill that there was something different about the super successful people. He knew a lot of them personally as well as a lot of ordinary people, and he knew they were different. He told him to go and study that difference. The thesis of the research became among others a world famous book entitled, 'Think and Grow Rich'.

It was not a book about thinking, and it was a book about exploring the world beyond our seeming physical limits; even beyond thought. That book takes you beyond thought into spirit.

Strange thing about that book'? There is nobody I know who is super-successful who has never read that book.

We have taught the 1% to pray.

Our prayers are therefore simply the 1% dust trying to touch spirit. It's pathetic. The answer from God comes, "Dust thou art and to dust thou shalt return."

Most of the prayers, placed under the microscope of digital analysis, reveal rather the practice of the absence of God than His presence.

A child asked his pastor one day if God was dead.

The pastor asked, 'Why do you ask?'

The little boys replied, 'You should listen to the people pray in church. It's like God is not listening, maybe gone on vacation'

We need to learn to pray as spirits.

The Athlete prays asking God to remove the zit on his face.

The Warrior prays that God should help him become this year's best sales rep in the country.

The States-Person prays for peace in the land; but the spirit asks for nothing, even though he spends the most time with God.

DRIVING DOWN 4TH BOULEVARD

I was driving down the N4 on my way home and the traffic was rather sinful. Most people switched on their pissed-off-gears.

Tempers and temperatures were getting higher as people stressed to get home earlier than the other road users. To think that most were rushing to unhappy homes or idle evenings - according to statistics - I wondered what the rush was all about.

I was driving to an empty home so I thought why I don't just enjoy driving as slowly as my car could, and I did.

When I resigned myself to enjoying what frustrated most people, poetry busted out my heart like an August storm; and it was all about me and how I came to be, and why I came to be and it went something like this:

(By the way I wrote it while I was driving on the congested N4 during peak hours. Driving down 4th Boulevard, as I said)

Son of Ecstasy

Me, I was formed in ecstasy, son of a pair of orgasms.
I hope being son of ecstasy means I am ecstasy reincarnate.
Hence will I my life in no other wise live;
Ecstasy being my sole signature.

When I look at the galaxy, milky at night, I see my trail.
The stars are none but the dust] left behind.
As I tore the skies blasting mine way
Towards my destiny in this incarnation.
The clouds are none but airbags scattered
Around to spare my then fragile bones.

The bright king of the skies,
the sun provided me with the might of wings.
While the moon was my candlelight,
guiding me through some candid nights.
So that miss none of the splendid views
that painted my stunning trail.

Now that I am here, traveller and traverser
of intergalactic space.
Inhabitant of a planet of dust,
terrestrial and extra-terrestrial a being.

I will do the least l can,
make dust in the world and leave a trail eternal behind.
And my ecstasy will I leave behind, testimony that l have been here.
Son of ecstasy, I insist!

Real Grown-ups know they appeared on earth urgently to fulfill an urgent mission. They know they are a mystery waiting to be revealed, a miracle Waiting to happen, and that time is running out and that they don't have forever in this incarnation.

They know they are a thing of beauty, a creation of a gazillion coincidences and their being here alone is a testimony to the fact they are special beings with special assignments.

"The illiterate of the 21st century will not be those who cannot read and write, but those who cannot learn, unlearn and relearn."
— *Alvin Tofller*

ONE

YOU CAN'T TEACH AN OLD DOG NEW TRICKS

Hello old dog; I am glad you've come thus far with reading this book. For an old dog you are not doing too badly.

I bet you feel old and doggy today.

I have bad news for you though, the old and doggy attitude is no longer allowed in this world. It was officially illegal the day when this book got an ISBN number and became a citizen of this country and by extension the world.

Doggitude is regarded as stupid and this country has adopted a zero tolerance attitude towards stupidity. Anybody and anything exhibiting stupid tendencies will be hauled to the dog house.

This was just an announcement.

If you don't get that, get this - learning is no longer an option, it is an imperative enforced by the law of Moses — this Moses.

In his book, "Future Shock", Alvin Toffler raises the standards.

The illiterate of the twenty first century will be defined only by the expectations and conditions of the twenty first century on mankind.

No less!

Whereas illiteracy in the twentieth century was defined as the inability to make head or tail of A and Z and everything in between. Twenty first century illiteracy will be much more linked to the ability to function rather than the ability to babble.

Changes in everything from technology to communication have become so rapid to keep up with the pace of the day one has to literally outrun oneself, and overtake your own vehicle in a way of speaking.

When you tell Grown-ups about new trends, new technologies, and new teachings, what is the common phrase you get?

"You can't teach old dogs new tricks."

Allow me to be harsh and blunt old dog, something I've been accused of on so many occasions it doesn't bother me anymore.

Firstly you are not a dog, and secondly learning is not a trick.

I know a dog is a man's best friend but should we extend the friendship that far, I don't think so.

One boring attribute about Grown-ups is the phobic suffix. If they are not claustrophobic they are technophobic, if not that they are just phobic, how pitiful.

You can't teach an old dog new tricks is the excuse you get when you try to give a bit of improvement and enlightenment to Grown-ups. These are the people who last saw a school classroom donkey years ago, but they still refuse to do any new learning, yet they still want to live on earth.

They have become relics of an antiquated education system.

First of all, the education you got was mostly not even relevant for your days. The education of most countries is still in the hands of the department of education which is mostly a bureaucratic organization that moves slower than trends.

Much, much slower.

So we can safely conclude that your education was obsolete even while it was being planned. How much more irrelevant do you think it is for the days in which you now live. To refuse to learn is the most stupid thing you will ever do in your life.

The following are the things I have personally observed with Grown-ups:

Computers? Too old.
Technology? Ted Nolan Who?
Internet? Inter what?

The only thing they will inter-rain is entertainment and inter course — a good course they don't offer at the University of Limpopo. Something that Adam invented and tried on the one guinea pig he got who was neither guinea nor a pig, buy a woman called Eve.

They were so good at it because it was their only occupation on earth after they lost the tender of tending to the garden from the Department of Agriculture and Environmental Affairs.

Some people think the naked pair lost the gardening project because they had intercourse. I say intercourse was on the menu. It was to be had.

It's the apples that were not on the six course meal:

Intercourse - starter,
Gardening - second starter
Intercourse- main meal
Gardening - the first dessert
Intercourse - final starter.

Or something like that. So intercourse was the interlude and the in-between break benefit of tending to the Garden. Stuff theologians!

The tree that was not supposed to be eaten was simply a tree.

I think it was weed or just weird. And Adam went high on that weed or that weird tree and when the high wore out; and he and his wife hit a huge hang-over, the mother of all babalaases.

Most Grown-ups seem to have inherited that babalaas for keeps.

Grown-ups must be having the mother of all hang-overs.

Pardon me for using mother, but hangovers happen too often to be orphans.

I am often tempted to think that drug pushers read the book of Genesis 3 a lot because the scenario between the naked pair, the snake, the tree, the promise of being cleverer than God, and the major losses that occur after the experiment is very similar to a drug pushing transaction.

Let me harshly repeat my answer to the question, 'You can't teach an old dog new tricks'.

Two answers -

Firstly you are not a dog.

You might think you are, your voice may not negate it, you might feel like one, you might have adopted some *doggitudes* as you went about your sojourn, but truth is - the naked truth at that (and do not read much into the naked thing you son of Adam and daughter of Eve) 'You. Are. Not. A. Dog'.

Niggas might call you dog, a sobriquet of endearment. If you are a man, women might call you that if you are too friendly to their species, but still you are not a dog. If you are a woman and you are loud mouth and take on the male species with words pound for pound you could be called a *bitch*, but I say, all that notwithstanding, you are still not a dog.

Secondly, learning is not a trick.

Trick-or-treat, that's Halloween and some dark magic. Learning is definitely not a trick. Karate probably, street wise manoeuvres perhaps, but definitely not learning. Therefore we must drop the old dog myth and prove our adulthood by admitting to ourselves we could never be too old to learn new things.

Australian, Peter Daniels, started primary school over again at the age of twenty six.

My cousin Joe, a year older than myself, went to primary school when I was doing high school. Two advantages. He was an A+ student thanks to his age, and he could wink at his female school teachers and they could feel the power of his wink.

Not that I think much of winks or that primary school teachers could be persuaded by one, I am just stating that my cousin had the greatest wink at school and he used it well.

For a primary school man he moved from winker to *winkist* (expert winker) in one year all by himself. Upheld our family name too.

What is wrong with Grown-ups? I ask yet again with a sense of irritation in my voice. Ain't nothing wrong with becoming a saint, but becoming a St Bernard? Hell no.

Let me take you on a journey to some adult cities of the world and I am not talking about Amsterdam, Holland here. I am talking about Seoul, Korea. Half of Seoul's adult population either attends a university or has graduated from one. South Korea has the highest number of PhD's per person in the world; and PhD's are mostly adults.

A couple of years ago, Korea was not on the map, we knew little about her, there wasn't much said about Koreans either, even their national soccer team made no strides. It was the Japanese that were spoken of, but Koreans were their poorer cousins.

Not for long, South Korea is emerging as a world power and one of the factors responsible for that is the fact they have the highest learning adult population in the world. They don't have old dogs in Seoul and learning is not regarded as a trick in South Korea. *Comprende?*

Matter of fact last time I checked, there are no old dogs in Korea.

They make sure of that by having them for dinner while they are still young. The short of it, no old dogs in Korea.

Am I accusing Grown-ups of letting their minds atrophy? Of course I am! As much as when people grow up they tend to allow mental declination. There is no scientific proof that the human brain should decline with age basically because the brain is not a mere physical organ, it is way more than physical. The brain is the communication hub between the human and the divine. That is why your spirit can't continue to exist if your brain dies.

The brain feeds on oxygen, the gas that is to *mankind* what gasoline is to *car-kind*. Lose your teeth and your hair, even more sad your libido, but do not lose your brain.

Even though your brain is small enough to be held in one hand, it is more than a thousand times more powerful than the world's most powerful computer. And computers are powerful and amazing. But remember the creature can never be more powerful than the creator. And as long as the brain has its diet of oxygen and glucose and lots of learning you are a man of fortune.

The following quote appeared in Fortune International in the 90's, "The most successful corporation of the 1990's will be called a learning organization".

In the same breath I would venture to say the most successful individual of our day and any day at all, would be a learning individual. Knowledge remains the main capital of today and tomorrow and those who shun it, will see no sunshine in their lives.

King Solomon, the man who was regarded as the wisest man who ever lived, says about himself, "I gave my heart to seek and search out by wisdom concerning all things that are done under heaven… And I gave my heart to know wisdom, and to know madness and folly…" He was not the wisest man in the world without reason.

In his study of wisdom he gave us the book of Proverbs.

In his study of madness he gave us the Songs of Solomon, for how can a man with a thousand wives write a poem and sing a song of true and singular love. How can a man with a thousand wives and over seven hundred concubines take any lady to the show, 'All you need is love'?

In his study of folly or stupidity he gave us the book of Ecclesiastes, because I believe it is the most stupid book ever written by any man, and a wise man *nogal*. It has its uses and I am sure it deserves its place in the canon but it is a stupid book. That's official!

Most people have thought so about it, but did not have the guts to say what I just said. Most of them fearing that God would strike them with lightning if they said it. Don't worry, God's other name is not Solomon, and the Bible? It was not faxed from heaven.

I know a lot of smart Grown-ups and a lot of stupid Grown-ups and as I converse with them, I have discovered several distinct differences. The smart ones read.

I know they do because they quote and recommend books and they read magazines, not your usual photographic types but magazines with hard content, but mostly it is books they read.

They read magazines because they have fresh content that keeps them in touch with trends. They don't want to be behind in anything.

When they hit the web it's not so they can catch up with the gossip or find out who is naked and nasty on Facebook and Instagram and what is the latest bawdy joke being circulated on twitter - or should I say *Black Twitter*.

The stupid ones either don't read at all, or they read stupid stuff.

When you ask them why they read, they say it's their pastime.

Passing time huh?

Life equals time and passing time is passing life and it is a very stupid thing to do.

These are clueless Grown-ups who watch the world evolve into greater forms while they are choking from the dust created by the hullabaloo. Old fools who have made careers out of stupidity.

Leaders who have never read Niccolo Michiavelli's 'The Prince' or Sun Tzu's 'The Art of War' or even ever heard of those men.

Preachers and pastors who only read the Bible.

The World today is moving at a pace faster than that of the days of the Apostle Paul and exclusively Pauline sermons soon become irrelevant. The twenty first century might soon find church obsolete and totally irrelevant. And if church is still lead by old dogs who don't want to learn, it will soon become the dog house instead of the God house.

I am talking about business leaders who do not know who Tom Peters is and have never read anything by Jack Welch. The only Jacks they know being Jack Daniels, the jackpot and a lot of jackasses.

Investors who have never heard of Warren Buffet or one Robert Kiyosaki. Black business men and Women Who have never read Chika Onyeani's "The Capitalist Nigger", no matter what opinion you take of it.

THE RISE AND FALL OF THE OLD DOGS

When I was a little boy the rich people in all black communities be it townships or rural areas were the general dealers. Everybody purchased every kind of commodity from them - ploughing tractors, seeds, groceries, underwear (some nasty, not sexy at all utilitarian undies, I must say), transportation, fuel, the works. Towns were far and theirs were the convenient stores of the day.

These men amassed fortunes for themselves and their families especially because their mark-ups were also enormous. But these men were not learners. They were old dogs that refused to learn any new trick.

They just kept busy and put their noses in the tills and none in any book of any kind. Some of them used to boast they were not educated but they were rich, and education was a waste of time. It seemed as if they were right, because the educated people around them were looking up to them in all ways, but wait a minute!

Around the early nineties transportation infrastructure improved.

More people began to have their own vehicles, while the faster business driven taxis joined the market. Crime also went to university and the security industry remained in primary school. The stupid old man who was the quintessential guard for all retail stores, Mr Flashlight, who could tell his boss the next day he dreamt the lotto numbers and still keep his job, became irrelevant as asset security.

Them old tigers continued to do what they used to do in the yesteryears. No change, no learning. Suddenly all of them as if hit by the bubonic plague began to get less and less busy. One by sorry one they began to fold. The stock in their shops became less and less. Some rented their shops to other stupid people who still thought owning a retail shop was the way to go, and never asked why the old businessman was so keen to retire.

The thing is, when a new idea hits the market, only the brave venture into it, the sceptics watch from a distance and criticise.

When the idea has fully run its course and has made its millionaires, it's then that the sceptics move in. They then burn their fingers to the bone and become even more sceptical than they had ever been. That is usually the life cycle of any economic rush. The rich become richer and the sceptics become more sceptical while the poor become poorer.

The early nineties where horrific. It was not nice to see yesterday's tycoons begging in the streets. Guys who used to be on top of the world now inhabitants of its armpits. It was the end of an era of once seemingly smart people now clearly stupid people.

You can't carry yesterday's smarts into today, neither can you carry today's smarts into tomorrow. Without continuous learning you risk becoming irrelevant.

If there is one thing you should never change when all things change is to continuously learn. It was General Eric Shinseki, Chief of Staff U.S Army who said, "If you don't like change, you're going to like irrelevance even less".

It is the non-learning Grown-up masses that pursue preservation instead of revolution. You see it in churches, the dullest brains, the most non-learning, and cling to old doctrines of ancient prophets who were hardly relevant even during their days. Any herald of a new future and ideals is persecuted as a heretic. The old order is doomed and they don't seem to have heard that. They still sing the *negro* spiritual, 'Give me that old time religion.' They value permanence - as yesterday so today.

In Tom Peters' words: "Permanence the last refuge of those with shrivelled imaginations."

Church is important to me because if you can remember clearly, as a Grown-up, after you have completed your formal education, church has become the only institution that creates a platform for the dissemination of ideas?

Church, at least once a week is the only remaining public arena for personal transformation. Problem with church is too many stupid people have chosen the ministry as a career. Too many stupid people who limit their reading to only one book are the only ones allowed to speak there.

I have a deal with God. If I can't find a progressive church with intelligent ministers who spend as much time in the library as they do in the closet; and are not afraid to be controversial, I will not go to '*His House*'.

I think it's a fair deal.

I would rather be planting tomatoes than visit a pretentious house of worship. Besides, God is not confined to buildings, he is everywhere. I could make it to heaven having never seen the aisle of a church.

Hey, enough about church, what about school as the other learning institution. There they teach by force. I had a lot of things throttled down my throat during my days. A couple of things I remember throttled down my throat during those days are:

The mathematical table — worth it, especially before the advent of the calculator;

The political geography of Africa and Eastern Europe — not worth it, because names of countries, presidents and borders changed like the weather any day.

Then there was, Jan van Riebeeck. He was huge; he was all of history. Allow me not to go further. I think I have a little bit of an issue with this one because it was throttled down our collective throats - Jan van Riebeeck.

WHO THE HELL IS JAN VAN RIEBEECK

When I Went to school they taught us that Jan Van Riebeeck came to the Cape in 1652 to establish a refreshment station, remember that?

This was said to be the foundation of South African History.

You were also never to forget that if you knew what was good for you. They taught me this version of history in standard three and five, and standard eight and ten.

When I went to the University of Limpopo I elected to study history. Before the first history class we were given a pre-lecture about the ratings of our history departments in the country. We were told that the University of Limpopo's was then the most highly rated history department in South Africa. I asked, 'Why', and we were told it was because of the academic standing of the personnel. The most junior member of staff was a professor with two Masters Degrees.

I went to attend the first class with great enthusiasm. An austere man came to class on the needle often, and introduced himself as a Professor Moolman.

He opened his educated mouth to give us the inaugural history lesson, and it went like this: "In the year 1652 Jan van Riebeeck came to the Cape to establish a refreshment s..."

That's all I ever heard him say because before he could finish his sentence, I had walked out of the history class never to return. It was the beginning of the school term so I went to find another subject.

I was *galvol* of Jan van Riebeeck.

Going back to primary and high school they taught us that a lizard doesn't have an ass it's got a cloaca. My take - a rose by any name still smells as sweet.

They told us how many eyes a locust had and how many legs. If you could remember all that, especially Jan van Riebeeck, you were an A+ student.

I have been through life and life has asked of me many a question. I've been around the *legendary* block but even as I speak, the Jan van Riebeeck question has not yet popped up.

It hasn't mattered whether he came to the Cape in 1652 or 1710, it hasn't mattered whether the names of his ships where Pinto, Panto and Punto. That education was just not good enough to help me face the challenges of life.

I have had to learn new things, more relevant things. I had to shun my education and comfort myself in that it had at least helped me acquire the skills of reading.

I went to school to become a teacher. I taught for nine months. When I changed careers into business I had to change my studies and my books.

Once in my life in the US of A, I bought an appliance business as well as a heat and air conditioning business. I had to enroll for a Mechanical Engineering degree. It was a three year course, but business imperatives compelled me to complete the degree in eight months. I was losing money because of insufficient knowledge. I burnt the midnight oil and that saved my life and my business.

Anytime my life has changed I have had to change my education and my books. I hate asking too many questions, learning is much easier. If you are learning though, even if you have to ask questions you ask the smart ones and the relevant ones.

Audit the content of your education or perhaps the content of your head and ask yourself one question, 'Who the hell is Jan van Riebeeck and how in hell is he going to put food on my table? 'He came to establish a refreshment station, but not in my house.

Audit the content of your head and if all you get is things that could have mattered years ago, that have now become irrelevant and obsolete, you are also by virtue of this stupid data occupying the prime piece of real estate above your shoulders, becoming irrelevant and obsolete too.

They say insanity is doing things the same way but expecting different result. So to change your results you have to change the way you do things. To change the way you do things you have to change the way you think. To change the way you think you have to change the data in your head and replace it with new data.

Replace Jan van Riebeeck with Jack Welch and then you are getting somewhere. Replace locusts with computers and then you are talking. Replace cloaca with ass, some kick-ass empowering knowledge and then we might even reach our highest calling.

'You can't teach an old dog new tricks' is wrong because no one can win today's wars with yesterday's weapons.

'You can't teach an old dog new tricks' is wrong because nobody can lead the pack today with yesterday's technology.

It is shameful to be a token leader of people who know better than you do in most things, in the name of being an old dog. It is a shame when your business and the market place asks you questions and all you can say is *woof, woof, woof!*

'You can't teach an old dog new tricks' is a stupid thing to say especially if the old dog is still going to seek residence on this earth. Old dogs who are not learning new tricks are soon going to become irrelevant dogs. You've got Jan van Riebeeck in your head and you think you are educated?

Ever since 1652 a whole lot of other people came to the Cape or anywhere for that matter to establish refreshment stations, get some intelligence on them, leave Jan alone. Jan is old news, Jan is tired, and his refreshment station is now a great city. Jan has done his part and for that I honour him. Just leave him the fart alone, will you?

John Holt, in 'How Children Fail', argues that "Since we can't know what knowledge will be most needed in the future, it is senseless to try to teach it in advance. Instead, we should try to turn out people who love learning so much and learn so well that they will be able to learn whatever needs to be learnt."

The blistering pace of change has set a retraining agenda for everyone, especially Grown-ups. Knowledge is the main capital of today and tomorrow's worlds.

When one looks out there in the economic arena, one observes that big corporations are spending more and more money on their employees, especially their most educated ones. We are all economic beings but the large corporations signify to us what a larger economic animal would look like.

These huge economic monstrosities feed on education and learning. If they don't learn they will disappear like dinosaurs did, if they become learning institutions they survive and grow.

What is good for the goose is good for the gander... as in the macrocosm so in the microcosm.

Lifelong education is now a dominant fact of life. Grown-ups must stop saying stupid things like 'You can't teach old dogs new tricks' and take their place at the forefront of charting the path to the new 'learning society'.

They must of course begin by stopping the fight over the TV remote control with their kids and lead by example. The ability to learn faster than your competitors may be the only sustainable competitive advantage you have left.

According to Robert Kiyosaki, the world has changed but education has not changed with it. According to Kiyosaki, children spend years in an antiquated educational system, studying subjects they will never use, preparing for a world that no longer exists.

Dr. Willard Doggett is quoted saying, "The world our kids are going to live in is changing four times faster than our schools. If our children are faced with such a challenge, what about their parents, the Grown-ups? If our children's education is antiquated what does that say about ours? I am not one for pity, but allow me to be pitiful. I pity old dogs.

"In three words I can sum up everything I've learnt about life; it goes on."
- *Robert Frost*

They say insanity is doing things the same way but expecting a different result.

So to change your results you have to change the way you do things. To change the way you do things you have to change the way you think.

To change the way you think you have to change the data in your head and replace it with new data.

TWO

IT'S TOO LATE, I'M TOO OLD

"It's too late" is a sad song that Dolly Patton sang. Still does. She is the only person I know who made lots of money singing those words. Everybody else must stay away from those four stupid words because they are some of the most impoverishing lyrics one could ever utter.

I know there are a lot of things that could have been done in the now, but people thought it was too late and resultantly those things were aborted.

It's too late is a song of fools because while you are still here you can do anything you want to do. You can still re-invent your life if you don't like its make, you can still multiply your factor, even the ways in which you exist.

Most people think it's too late to do anything, especially the important things. Too late to change careers, too late to go to school, too late to relocate, too late to change churches, too late to change course, too late to move on, too late to start afresh, starting afresh in anything, including marriage.

If you were driving somewhere and suddenly you realise you are going in the wrong direction, would you just continue on that path or would you change direction?

Life is a journey, but most people upon realising they are headed in the wrong direction, either just slow down or just drive on. It's simply stupid to continue on the wrong path with all your faculties involved, but people do it anyway.

I am personally guilty of that too.

During my university days, I knew as soon as the first month had transpired that studying education was not for me and that the subjects I had taken were wrong for me, but I did nothing about it.

Yes it would have been a challenge to start afresh and do something of which I had no preparation in matric, but it would have been better than wasting time studying in a field that was not appropriate for me. I was afraid that my parents back home would disagree with my change of path but I never tried to engage them.

Looking at it now, if I had really sat with them and put my case across convincingly, them having been teachers, would have understood. But that was the one stupid thing a young person did. God forbid that as a Grown-up I repeat the same mistake. That would be inexcusable.

Of course someone might argue that it happened the way fate would have had it. I would say, 'who the hell is Fate?' Some fairy autocrat controlling my life without my consent. Atheists say God is dead, I say it's Fate who is, not God. I attended his funeral years ago, I should know.

Let's look at careers because they serve a good example of life paths, and they are probably life's greatest preoccupation and occupation. I tell you what, statistically more than 80% of the people of the world choose wrong careers and only find out a bit later in life.

Some people choose wrong careers because their families were not able to afford them the kind of education that goes with their preferred careers. Others because they come from places of total non-exposure. I mean places like where I born and bred.

My exposure to careers was, a large gallery of teachers, one policeman, one traffic cop, one thief (kept the one police man pretty busy but was always sure to be found because he mostly stole beer and would down a couple of bottles at the crime scene. A couple of bottles later he would be transformed into a gospel musician of the 'Moruti Ndlovu genre', academically unclassifiable that is, and he would begin to sing vociferously not quite from his diaphragm, mostly from his sinuses — some squeaky throaty Z minor vocal trash).

Other professionals (And I am being soft on the word professional) included a shopkeeper (mostly victim of the one thief) and a visiting priest who devoured enough eggs to make even pythons envious.

Not even one dirty lawyer. That is if lawyers are really dirty.

I remember telling a Grown-up cousin of mine a long time ago as a child that I wanted to become a lawyer. He told me how lawyers were liars and how they were all going to hell. I backed off. The stories I had heard about hell that time were so graphically horrific I knew to stay away. Fire, brimstone, wailing, gnashing of teeth, abject thirst and the works.

Later in life I only discovered that second to a dog, a good lawyer might just be a man's best friend. Also that hell as I knew it, was probably an embellishment by evangelical *pulpiteers*, of a subject of little focus by bible writers. A tool for preachers who lacked the ability and imagination to persuade men towards the knowledge of God through positive means. Pulpit bullies with nothing but hot wind behind their words.

There are many and varied reasons why people choose wrong or second choice careers. Of those only about 20% go back and correct the mistake. This 20% becomes very successful while those who do not change resign themselves to becoming abject failures.

A friend of mine was talking to his wife who was then about thirty years old. The wife had always wanted to become a doctor.

He said to her, "Why don't you give it a shot?"

She said, "You see, it takes seven full years. Seven years from now I will be thirty seven, I would be too old".

He said to her, "So? If you don't study in seven years you will still be thirty seven, but you won't be a doctor".

The man had a point.

Say these words after me, I might be old, but I am not leaving this world without applause. I might be old, but I am still here breathing and I might be old, but the universe has still invested a good puff of oxygen in me; and if I am deserving of the life-force, I deserve to give life and its Mount Everest a shot.

I might be old, but l am in, not on my way out!

I heard someone say, I think it was the Namey called Fran; "If you are going to die, be drop-dead" (As in drop-dead gorgeous). I concur. Can I concur? I may be wrong but I think if anybody, I have earned the right to concur. As a Grown-up I believe in earning my place in life, it's the Grown-up thing to do.

Cyril Ramaphosa started as a lawyer. He changed. I started as a teacher, I changed in nine months. Nthato Motlana started as a medical doctor but later became arguably the number one black businessman in the country during his day. M.K. Mohlala, former CEO and President of City Power started out as a security guard. Ray McCauley of Rhema was a bodybuilder, later he was the builder of a much larger body, the body of Christ.

IN MY TIME...

Another way 'It's too late', is expressed by grown-downs who pretend to be Grown-ups is, 'In my time'. What the hell is that, 'In my time...'?

As long as you are still able to articulate those words it's your time, except of course if you are talking about playing professional football at fifty, that might not be your time.

As long as God still gives you breath, it is your time, shut up and do just more than breathe. I think people who say such things as "In my time" are pathetic, except of course for Teddy Pendergrass who made a lot of money repeating those words.

I think some people should go around with tombstones on top of their heads inscribed with the words, "In loving memory of our beloved brother Sello. He died ten years ago, just that instead of getting buried he got married. He has maintained a vertical position with regulated motion but everything about him is horizontal. He is greatly missed by all his family and the maggots of the deep under. Rust in piece."

Did I tell you the story of the tourist during the last solar eclipse who asked an elderly dude in Polokwane a question typical of tourists? Tourists, often ask questions that kindergarten kids would regard as way below their station or even condescending.

Tourist: "Have you lived here all your life?"

The old Polokwanian: "Not yet."

Good answer…

Don't behave like you are a subject of history books. While you are still on earth it is very necessary to live whatever there is of your life.

When you look back at your life and reminisce, your mind tells you, 'You had your times.' Maybe you did. And I hope we are not talking about the discos you attended and the late nights and the hangovers.

As you look back at your so-called good times, Virgil would say, "Meanwhile, time is flying . Flying never to return".

When I was a teenager I played football, a prolific striker with blistering pace who scored many a vital goal for all my teams in those days. At the age of seventeen I played for the Ipopeng High School A-Team. It was a hard team to make. But soon after I got in I left football in pursuit of a God that I thought had no bone for sport in his body.

I became a Mzalwana (born again Christian)

One stupid *Mzalwana* told me that while I was busy chasing the soccer ball, souls were dying. I was young and impressionable and so he got to me. I quit soccer immediately.

When I left football I was a star already. I had already been scouted by the then Mahwelereng Motherwells, later Real Rovers.

But stupid religion had got to me and there was no one around to rescue me. I went to university for five years and never played football during that period.

At the age of twenty three while a lecturer at Kwena Moloto College I was approached by two scouts from Ria Stars. Then they were still in the second division. They told me their team wanted me. My answer to them was, 'I am too old.' Can you imagine. In my time I was stupid enough to utter such words.

At that time having been through university, I knew God had no beef with football. I knew I could play sports and still serve Him, but something else was stuck in my brain — the thought that it was too late. Where that quick answer came from, the answer that relegated me farther away from the world of sports, and blew off my second chance at life in the world of professional sports I don't know.

Twenty three years old. Too late?

What the heck was that? Where did the stupid phrase spring from'? If I had played professional soccer I would have been better known, and selling my books would have been a whole lot easier. Every talent you have enhances the others.

So my advice to you is that you should pursue a multi-talented life-style, that way you can even synergize with your own self. That is what Christ would call abundant life.

What is teeming in your brain that you want to pursue? Are you hearing the voice in your brain saying, 'It's too late?' Exorcise the little demon because it is not true. The day they sing, 'Nearer My God Nearer To Thee', and lower the coffin to the gaping hole deep under. And the body in the coffin is the one you used to inhabit, only then, and only then is it too late. Before that, just shut up and continue with the grand pursuits of your life.

It's too late is a stupid song sung by old fools. How can you say it's too late while the sun is still warming your body? How can you say it's too late while your body is still heaving with breath?

How can you say it's too late when those words are not your final words? How can you say it's too late when you have already learnt so much? How can you say it's too late when you have before you more resources than you have ever had in your life? How can you say it's too late when you are a Grown-up ?

IT'S TOO LATE TO SAY IT'S TOO LATE

As a Grown-up you must admit, it's too late to say it's too late.

An adult must transform his life - pull himself up by his own bootstraps. If he can't he must expose himself to people and environments where transformation is possible, even natural. Volunteer yourself to change.

The holy book says, "In the beginning was the word... and nothing was formed or created except by the Word". So the same force of creation is also the force of transformation.

The spoken word, the written word, the silent word - that voice that emanates from the meditative mind — these are forces that can change an 'it's too later' into a creator. In my life I have experienced goose bumps when I saw how forceful the spoken Word is in human transformation.

I've seen turn-arounds during some of my speaking engagements that made me think that the ministry of prophets has not retired.

Somebody asked me one day if I was still praying for the healing of the sick. I used to. I have seen lunatics become sane, demons getting exorcised and cancer being healed, barren wombs being able to bear children and a lot of other things happening, and I am not trying to sound like a mystic or anything. This guy asked if I was still doing that.

Healing people that is. While the healing ministry is still of value, what's the point in healing people and they are still stupid. I said, 'Occasionally but not much anymore'.

He asked why? I said, 'I think the demons I am now exorcising are the demons of the mind'. They can be stubborn too, but when you observe those cured from such, you marvel how great the potential for achievement in humans is. I used to heal the body and I still can, but what is the body but dust.

It is the saving of souls and that, not in a religious way - that is the higher calling.

We had the Elijah's, Elisha's, Jeremiah's, Emersons, Confucius, Thoreau's and Martin Luthers, who brought revolution to their generations and beyond.

Fiery men who spoke as if possessed. Indeed they were possessed. By themselves. Their higher selves. Their invisible selves. Sometimes we look back and think it was all history. I say we still have our prophets in our day and this particular one (self-aggrandizement not intended) is saying to you, 'No matter how old you are, it's not too late.'

Their words will give you a major turn-around and you can cover up for lost years if you can hearken to the voice of the divine through them. We have modern day prophets whose ministration of inspiration cannot be ignored and I am not speaking in a religious context.

In my life I have been impacted by Phillip Hlungwani and Deepak Chopra, I have eaten out of the hands of Wayne Dyer and Eckhardt Tolle, I have been lifted by the words of Tom Peters and I have marveled at the mighty lines of Wole Soyinka.

I listened to Oprah Winfrey interviewed and the latent water in my ocular glands gave in to gravity. I have also been greatly moved by a now silent prophet, Rev Frank Chikane.

People say I am an orator. I say to them you should listen to Frank Chikane. If he is not speaking any more, get one of his old tapes. I can never forget his oration on 'The Role of the Church'. The wisdom, the beauty, the poetry — awesome! These people do not have to be Christians or Muslims or Hindus or Sufis. They just have to be prophets of the one divine force.

They are bigger than labels because the divine force cannot be categorized. There are no labels in the garden of mystics.

While Abraham was still trying to find God and categorize Him, he was visited by a man who came from nowhere, a dude called Melchizedek, King of Salem. A man of God who could not be categorized. I am sure the message that Melchizedek carried to Abraham was - 'God Is a No-Name Brand. Why pay more, for just a name'. Raymond Ackerman is a smart guy and we all know it.

It is category that is the greatest enemy of progress in finding enlightenment, and the greatest victims of categorization the world over are Christians. From Orthodoxy to Catholicism, from Catholicism to Protestantism. From Evangelicals to Pentecostals, from Pentecostals to Charismatics, and from Charismatics to whatever is next, something the so-called controversial voices of the 21st century seem to be heralding.

When I talk about paying for a name I am talking about all the blood that was shed because of names, *God, Allah, Jehovah, Krishna, Modimo, Unkulunkulu*, etcetera, etcetera!

Among Christians, everybody believes everybody is lost just because of a singular interpretation of a verse of scripture that in ten different translations does not even mean the same thing.

Majoring in minors, we pass God on our way to church, and while in there, we wallow in the mud of our own religiosity and call the freak-out, the experience of God. A God who we missed at the corner of a street, next to the local tavern. 'Prophet-ing' is not over yet because God has not lost interest in the human race no matter how messed up we are.

It cannot be over because we are still all sent here as packages of mystery waiting to be unpacked, and such is the work of these people I call prophets — often to help us unpack ourselves and show us in the way we should go.

While God is still on the throne, which will forever be, his voice will continue to be heard and it will be heard from the mouths of men. Remember the biblical parable of 'The Rich Man and Lazarus'.

The rich man went to hell after he died.

There while in great pain he asked Father Abraham, in fact screamed at him because he was in a different place.

He said to Abraham, "Please send somebody to earth to go and warn earthlings especially my brothers that they have responsibilities and that they should execute them while they are still alive".

Abraham's indifferent answer was: "We are not sending anybody from here, because they have Moses and the Prophets. They should listen to them. If they don't, they wouldn't listen to anybody form here or from anywhere".

You know why'? Because Moses and The Prophets are from there anyway. Incidentally, I am Moses. So read on brother!

Peter J Daniels heard the voice of inspiration while listening to Dr Billy Graham. At that time in his life he was like a ship without a rudder in a thick fog.

He was direction-less, illiterate, very poor, very bitter and seemingly without a future (too late, somebody might have thought), and he was 27 years old and that was in 1959.

Whatever the fiery prophet articulated that day I do not know, but it triggered a series of activities in Peter Daniel's life that landed him where he is today. A man of great learning and intellect. A philosopher and educator in his own right, one of the world's highest paid motivational speakers, a business leader with ventures in over 127 countries, a debt free multi-millionaire, prolific author and provocative speaker.

Before he met this prophet it looked as though for him it was too late. But was it? I met one of my kinsmen at a funeral who I had last seen a few years back.

The last time I had seen him he was driving an old Opel Rekord that was so ailing it ought to have been bumper *stickered* 'FOR MECHANICS ONLY'.

A good mechanic, he coped, with greasy hands. But this time when I met him I could hardly recognize the man. He was emerging out of the latest Mercedes Benz dressed in Italian cotton.

He saw me and sped to me with great joy "I've been looking for you for ages just to thank you." "For what?" I asked.

He said: "For making me meet your friend Phillip Hlungwani. "Remember his speech that day? It changed my life completely.

I was a hardworking man going nowhere, a slave of poverty. But that day my life took a mighty swing. Now I can afford what my heart desires. When you meet him again please tell him to keep on the good work. Please thank him for me." And Phillip had only been speaking at a wedding. There had been more love in his talk than business motivation.

However, the speech still transformed a guy whose life looked as though it was too late to turn around. Phillip and I and a business associate and friend of ours, Solly Matjekane used to hold motivational sessions at Limpopo's major hotels. These seminars affected many lives in a positive way.

I have no fear when I say that we were standing in the offices of prophets. (Not in a religious sense though). What came out of those meetings was mind-boggling. People were being swayed from the mundane life of career chasing to the higher path of following their star, their destiny.

The last of these meetings was held at Venda Sun with the theme, 'WHY YOU HAVE WORKED SO LONG, HANDLED SO MUCH, BUT STILL LACK AND HAVE NOTHING'.

Out of these meetings people's directions in life changed drastically. Transformation and creation of new lives took place on a massive scale. 'A dental surgeon who was working for the civil service in a public hospital took a giant leap. She did the thing she was always postponing into the distant foggy future. She quit the hospital and opened her own dental surgery. It was so successful that in less than a year she was already the proprietor of two.

When I talked to her, she said she made her resolve and gathered her guts during the last of our meeting she had attended.

'A teacher left the classroom for a marketing job. In a few years he had changed the place of his abode twice for better. I met him just after he had bought himself a new car. He attributed his new strides in life to the inspiration he got from our sessions. He had never missed a session ever since we started.'

'One other guy, a teacher; did not quit his job. He was running a side-line business which boomed and expanded after these sessions to an extent he started making more money in a week selling live chickens than he was fetching from his job in a month. I suspect chickens could take offence at me applauding the success of a man who was selling their kind to be devoured by another two legged species.'

I do console myself in knowing that chickens cannot read this book. If not even half the population of humans is going to ever read this book in my lifetime no matter how successful it becomes, how much of a chance do chickens have.

The greatest lovers of chicken, us - black people are the worst in this regard. The day chickens begin to read, the reading population of the world's race to the book could stand at:

1. White people and
2. Other races
3. Chickens and
4. You know who.

If you don't believe me go to Exclusive books anywhere in the country. While there, count how many black people are there at any given time. Then count the white people. Then remember that the white to black ratio in this country is 87% to 13% almost.

I did this count for five weeks in a row. The average is 90% white and 10% black. So black people, chickens are gaining in on us. Before we think about it, chickens would be smart enough to eat us. Well everybody else has. Read the Capitalist Nigger if you don't believe me.

Is it really too late or you just have been thinking so? I don't think so. Change what you are listening to, change what you are reading and change who you hang out with. You might just be thinking it's too late because you are hearing the wrong stuff.

Change your church too because after your school days, the church seems to be the only place where people gather to hear positive stuff. A church that tells you of your sinful nature and of heaven as a goal for Christian faith is not good for you.

A church that is big on hell is just as bad because nobody can really convince me that the purpose of living is to avoid hell and go to heaven. Then I would join King Solomon and rant —'Vanity of vanities, all is vanity!' No matter how high heaven is, you need to hear stuff that will make your earthly sojourn a great experience despite how lowly some men of the cloth might regard it.

I would rather be an usher in a church that transforms my life than an elder in a church that accuses me of sin I have not committed — Adam's sin.

Who the hell is Adam?

I have beef with him, his girlfriend Eve and Jan van Ricbeeck.

"Whatever else we are, no matter how much of a mess we have made of our lives, it is always possible to tap into the part of the soul that is universal, the infinite field of pure potential, and change the course of our destiny."
 - *Deepak Chopra*

It's too late is a stupid song sung by old fools. How can you say it's too late while the sun is still warming your body?

How can you say it's too late while your body is still heaving with breath?

How can you say it's too late when those words are not your final words?

How can you say it's too late when you have already learnt so much?

How can you say it's too late when you have before you more resources than you have ever had all your life?

How can you say it's too late when you are a Grown-up ?

THREE

THE FEAR OF CHANGE

Most Grown-ups are employees, about 80% of us. Because being an employee takes most people's awake minutes, we have suddenly become life's employees in all of life. We live our lives in employee mode even after hours.

Rude awakening?

You are not an employee in your own life. You are not like a person who works for a huge conglomerate where you can't change things when they don't work. In your life, an organization called, 'You Incorporated'.

You are the boss.

The main man. When you reflect upon your life, do you think there are things that need to change?

If there are, I have good news for you. You don't have to consult anybody about it. Not your boss, not your spouse, not your children. Not even your God.

Most people have become very little in life because they think they should go to God about everything in their lives. My daughter only comes to me when she is totally stuck, when she can't help herself. When all is well she just comes to me to love me and be loved by me.

In my book, most of what we call prayer today is totally unnecessary, especially loud public prayer. I have heard a lot of stupid unnecessary mumbo-jumbo masquerading as prayer. I have seen people open and close ceremonies in prayer, inviting God to meetings which he himself convened or meetings he would never attend.

I have heard people shout at God like he was deaf and mumble at him like He was mean. "Oh Father God as we start this service we pray that you will be in our midst."

He said, "Where two or three gather in my name I will be in their midst." What of that did you not understand? I am talking about prayers like, "Oh Lord, please anoint the preacher and let it be you who speaks through him". If your speaker hasn't got the stuff, you can shout all night, that anointing ain't happening.

If your speaker is stupid, God is not going to speak through him lest he be confused with stupidity. Bottom line, I have heard a lot of stupid prayers in my life. What I am saying is, "Leave God alone, he has given you all the faculties and all the resources. Just get stuck in and change your own circumstances".

Change is an inevitable part of our existence. Even God changes things around when they don't work. The scripture that says, 'I am the Lord and I change not', simply means 'I am the Lord and I do not give change'. Have you ever seen a person put a Hundred Rands in the offering basket in church and take back fifty? I have seen a Chinese policeman in Mamelodi even, but I have never seen something like that happening.

Just following the Jews' pursuit of their highest selves, Abraham, a pagan, who was himself not a Jew moved from paganism to Monotheism which later became Judaism. Judaism gave in to Christianity and I believe that Christianity is about to give birth to something else, something much more inclusive and much more powerful.

A better version of itself which might still maintain the same label, yet labels will slowly become immaterial.

There is going to be an interlinking of religions, even a merging, as people become enlightened and awaken to the fact that God whom we've given multiple names is just the one God. Labels will fall away and become insignificant.

On this one I am not pleading the Fifth Amendment. I would rather hide behind the words of Thomas Huxley that says — 'It is the customary fate of new truths to begin as heresies'

Wasn't it Jesus himself who said, "Greater works than these shall they do ..." Indeed it was him. But I believe that just mentioning the above statements will send a shock wave among Christians just like the *Da Vinci Code* did. But that's just because there is no open-mindedness in religion, and when Christianity becomes a religion it suffers the same fate as other religions.

Let me make one thing clear, before anybody can do greater things than the things Jesus did, he must have been able to raise himself by his own bootstraps if you will, to a place of equality with Jesus. How can you surpass someone that you are looking up to?

A few things I believe would happen if Jesus came back to earth in a reincarnation similar to the first. He would be born in Africa, probably in Zimbabwe. Mugabe would try to kill him. He would be taken to America where he would lie low until the end of the Mugabe regime.

He would come back to Africa but choose to live in South Africa mostly because of the rich music and rich culture of intellectual debate and relative tolerance of differences. (South Africans are the only people in the world who have held talks about talks — CODESA)

He would disassociate himself with most of what is called church and it would be Christians not the Jews who would crucify him this time around.

He would specifically treat some Christian groups the way he treated the Pharisees and the Sadducees. He would speak pretty much like me and he would be called controversial.

CHANGING RELATIONSHIPS

Let me not deviate from turn-around strategies. Yes everybody needs an ever-oiling turn-around mechanism if you want results and success.

People stay in bad marriages, cheat on their partners and live miserable lives and make life miserable for their kids and when you ask them why they are not moving on and out of their miserable relationships they tell you because God hates divorce.

Three things: Firstly, God is not married. Shamefully I read a book that said that God was once married to thirteen thousands wives and he loved them equally. I didn't think much of it because having experienced the bliss of contact with Him I didn't think he would want female or male companionship to be God.

God is everything there is.

He created us in his own image yet we keep creating him in our own image. He creates and has created all there is. In him there is joy, peace, bliss, happiness, ecstasy, everything.

Secondly, God is not married to your spouse so it is not up to Him. And, thirdly, God hates other things two. Like two miserable people living together and increasing each other's misery.

I am not preaching a doctrine of divorce at all. A lot of ailing marriages can be healed, but there are those that can't, period. Just like there are incurable diseases and untenable situations there are marriages that can't be saved and in such a situation it is the individuals who need to be saved even from each other.

My argument here is based on the fact that certain people's coming together could be a mistake. So you are either going to try to improve on a mistake or get out of it and start afresh. If you were building a house and you discover cracks in your foundation what are you going to do?

Continue to build? That would be Stupid!

If you think yours has a chance then go and see a counsellor, although most of the times the counselling route is usually the doorway out of the marriage. Reason being there is usually a reluctant partner being dragged to the counselling session.

Remember, a man convinced against himself is of the same opinion still. If you remain in one of those marriages that may never work you will never be productive, you will live as a spiritual dwarf and die as one. It is hard to rise above your most basic of relationships. Bad husbands or wives make bad fathers and mothers mostly, and in the real true spirit of achievement they will always underachieve.

When I talk under-achievement I am talking as compared to no other person but yourself. Just because you do better than your neighbour does not mean you are an achiever.

WHAT ABOUT FRIENDS?

Show me a man's friends and I will show you how far he will go in life. If I audit your cell phone bill, your five most frequently dialed numbers will tell me volumes about who you are.

I am cool with being a friend of the world and acknowledging the divinity in every man, but I am not cool with spending the most of my sacred moments with people who would deduct from me. I therefore do not associate with:

- People who don't read
- People who spend their time judging others and saying all manner of ill about others
- Old dogs who 'Trick-orTreat'
- People who are afraid to raise a finger in fear of what people would say.

There are many others, but if you are characterised by those, you will definitely deduct from me. But mostly I stay away from people who refuse to learn and change.

Yes, I change friends like I change underwear.

You want to change an underwear before it develops a flavour, which is daily. So if a friend begins to leave a bad taste in your mouth order a strong drink, like two tots Listerine on the rocks and spit them out with it.

Life is too short.

CHANGE YOUR ENVIRONMENT OR IT WILL CHANGE YOU

Another great subject of change in life if you want to leave this world in applause is your environment. I was not born in Pretoria but I went there as quickly as I could.

What I want to do, is change the world and I wanted an environment and a place where I would be able to do that quicker and more effectively than anywhere else.

Time is short.

I am not looking down at Ramalapa, the place where I was born, it's a great place and I am partly what I am because of it. However, if I stayed there for all my allocated time on earth I would not be able to achieve all I need to achieve. I love my mother tongue but if I wrote solely in *Sotho* there would be a limit to the numbers of people I could reach.

Before I am a Sotho man I am a man with a divine mission.

God's understudy.

I want that when I go to the next incarnation or non-carnation, to be able to account for all the years of my life with deeds of great impact. I do not want to say to Him I was a great village man, a *Phiri* (village grave digger).

In my opinion every village must invest in an earth moving vehicle for the digging of graves, let village men be assigned some greater tasks. Tasks that will shape and change the world in their time.

It matters not how many graves you dig and how many people you buried, what matters is what are you going to leave behind, when your number comes up.

Maybe I should give you a piece of myself by letting you in on the place where I come from. Little has been written on this interesting village. If I am not mistaken I am the first and only person who has written about Ramalapa in a published work of literature, the following is an extract from my so-called controversial novel, 'For Thine Is the Kingdom'.

This is the portion where I write about the village that gave birth to me and raised me. This should provide you some relief from my pungent attack of your way of life. 'Enjoy it.'

Ramalapa, a name which becomes important to the narration of our story is a village situated about forty-five to fifty kilometers from the City of Polokwane, capital of Limpopo, depending on which route you decided to take.

Whatever route you took to this village you had better be driving a tough and high clearance vehicle. The people of this village, though important in their own estimate of themselves, never had citizens with enough political clout whether during the old Bantustan days or the new freedom days.

Therefore they waited for donkey years for politicians to stretch the tarred road their way but in vain. From that unfortunate settlement it seemed as though the civil engineer with the road infrastructure would show up a couple of days after Jesus' second coming. If Jesus was coming at all, these engineer fellows were going to show up soon thereafter. Being religious, the people of Ramalapa could wait for the civil engineer since they had been waiting for one greater with less proof.

Ramalapa itself was a village of people who took themselves a little too seriously. They believed without much mention that their village was the navel of *Matlala*, in spite of the dusty roads and the absence of tar. According to them the Chief Maurne Matlala elected to build his abode on the mountain so that he could be able to worship down the river at the shrine which was their village.

The Chief did unknowingly pay homage to this vain homestead by coming regularly to their graduation parties, which were numerous. There the Chief spoke in deep Elizabethan English that would have baffled both Queen Elizabeth and Shakespeare combined, not for flair and flavour but for the concentration of verbosity it possessed. All the neighbouring villages were gnawed by the worm of envy as they beheld these *unfoldings*. Those who resented this even the more went about telling how illegitimate Maume's chieftainship was.

They told stories of how he came back from Soweto where he grew up to murder people in the succession line so he could be the Chief. The stories were many and varied and they were embellished each time they were told, and gained on the dramatic as they were narrated by those who were rich of tongue. The only constant in them was that Maume was not the rightful Chief of the Matlala tribe, simply an impostor shining in borrowed robes.

The Ramalapa people were small with such tales because in many ways he was still their Chief. He also sipped expensive Scotch whiskey with the elite of the village and spoke English with them.

He liked these folk because in all his clan if it were really his, this was the only village which could appreciate a chief who spoke like Macbeth or Shakespeare's Caesar.

Although the villagers of this anointed homestead took themselves rather gravely, *Ramalapans* had their comic side too, and it was this side of them that made them rather interesting. In spite of the multiplicity of their social deviants, they were the most educated and graduated village in the whole of western Polokwane. Some statistician of dubious qualifications even ventured to claim that they had more university graduates per square meter than anywhere in the country.

Credit here should be given to the mission of the Church of England and the Holy Roman Catholic Church', the statistician emphasized with rumour written all over his face. The funny thing about it was that most of their learned citizens were also religious and elders in those two churches, but the same were also wanton drunks. In their drunken stupors they spoke the sweetest, decorous and most educated specimen of the English language extant in those parts of the world, which they were famous for.

Their spoken English was verbose and littered with some real bombastic words of great fancy. They spoke in fine sentences and choice phrases. People who were generous in the sharing of their bodies were called philanderers and those who spoke freely about such things were called slanderers in that part of the *world*.

Choice words indeed.

Contrary to opinions held elsewhere, the lunacy of Ramalapa was not the sole province of its lunatics. It was the general plague of the society that was spread evenly per square mile, like influenza during its season. It was in the air, in the way they socialized, in the way they the gossiped, in the way they celebrated the exploits of their deviants, and rumoured the sexploits of their philanderers through their slanderings.

It was in how they seemed to rejoice at and celebrate their drunks.

They had quite a spread of weird drunks by behaviour.

They had the worst kinds in the entire region. There was one who defecated himself when the booze was good and aplenty. There was the lady, if the good English people might be generous and allow us to call her so, who opened the floodgates of Urinia - Urinia being the undiscovered planet whose force presses onto human bladders and cause the whole fauna to excrete - *Pedi* mythology - after a couple of wine glasses with unrivalled consistency. And the one who passed out into fits of near death experiences after simply smelling the sweet flavour of the booze.

The latter was rumoured to have mothered a child whose sire was utterly unknown to her. Worse in that she was at that time, so she believed, sexually inactive. A very disappointed grandsire appropriately named the child Virginia, after the Immaculate Conception.

Then there were the two brothers who toured the world of the mentally damned and became total mad men under the influence of liquor. The same denizens of psycho mania sobered the next morning into the most decent of citizens.

The twain had a neighbour who on debut took such a trip and the poor tourist never returned to the shores of sobriety and by association sanity.

Then there was the school inspector who was a guest of one of the high society families with a matrimonial interest in their very beautiful daughter, who did the dumbest of things.

He tarried a wee bit at the bottle of a highly matured scotch whiskey enjoying the company around and passing time like a conveyor belt. As it often happens he went in and out the bathroom staggering in that matured and educated way, amusing his party as he went about.

It was when he went to the lavatory for the fifth time that he looked a lower specimen of man. He looked like a bird learning to fly. His hands were outstretched while he was trying to feel the walls around like a drunken blind martial artist.

He did make it to the house of excretion and made contact with the planet Urinia. There he unbuckled and unzipped, as he later narrated to his colleague who had married into the self-same family, in their ever so charming English.

"I took out my weapon of mass construction, and lo and behold they were twain. I thought there was something wrong with my eyes, so I rubbed them ever so thoroughly and limpidly by reason of the booze got a steadier stance and gazed ever so intently at familiar pipe, but they remained a stubborn pair. I then got a bit frightened and thought if I would let them both do the pressing and needful thing I could splash the floor and scandalize my learned name."

"So I judiciously decided to let go of one of the monsters, self-flattery not intended. I manhandled it ever so carefully making sure that I have a full grasp thereof and shoved it safely back into its habitat. Then l looked up the ceiling to enjoy man's third pleasure as thoroughly as I could."

"I opened the floodgates of my male-ness and the release was most liberating. Free at last, free at last. Thank God ouch! That was when I felt kind of warm - some dejavu warmth that I remembered feeling way back during my formative years."

It was when the warmth became intensely comforting that I realised what had just happened. I realised I had put the wrong monster back into the cage. My next mission was to take it out quickly and exchange it for the right one. My hands were too slow by reason of the booze because just when I was able to grab it, the damage had been done. I shamefully pulled my pants up and wobbled my way to sit shamelessly with the rest of the educated party."

"*Them* snobs, they just looked at me with accusing finality.

I knew right then that I would never be able to take their daughter's hand in marriage."

At this stage his friend, another Shakespearian who had listened with quiet interest, laughed so loudly the narrator couldn't help but join in the spontaneity. When the laughter had abated he said with a voice akin to that of Shakespeare's Hamlet in Hollywood, "To pee or not to pee, that is the question."

They joined again in laughing abandon.

I will nevertheless close this excerpt with one of John Payne's most quoted sayings - "Mid pleasures and palaces though we may roam, Be it ever so humble, there is no place like home."

ENVIRONMENT, ENVIRONMENT, ENVIRONMENT

Michelangelo was a sculptor, a rising star when he caught the eye of one Lorenzo de' Medici, the richest banker in Europe. He took him to his palace, clothed him in velvet and made him to dine with his son. At that princely table of the man who was called 'The Magnificent' where poets and scholars clustered, readings replaced common-day chatter.

Here the youth heard the great thoughts of Plato, the mighty lines of Dante. A second talent - poetry was inspired out of him - he was to become the author of seventy-seven sonnets.

I remember when l grew up that the greatest teacher I ever had in my life was one Mrs Constance Kgomo of Ramalapa, may the

Lord rest her soul. She had the greatest impact in my life while I was just in my primary school, Ramalapa Primary. They were rich and my family was poor then. She made it a point that after school I come to her house to spend time in her library reading books, and associating with her children.

I was also one of the few privileged to watch Liverpool and Manchester United on her TV, the first television in the village.

She wanted to expose me to English soccer, higher standards, and acquaint me to bigger books than the ones we were exposed to at school.

I know I owe a lot of what I have become to that great teacher.

She understood environment. She understood environment so much that she pulled out all stops to make it a point that I had the added if not right influence. She was one of my guardian angels, my angel of learning.

Moses the deliverer of the Israelites had to be raised in the courts of the great Pharaoh if he was to be able to stand up to another Pharaoh. Coincidence after coincidence saw to it that he is raised as a prince.

A prince who would be known as Moses, Conqueror of Ethiopia, Beloved of the Nile gods. By the way coincidence is simply God's own way of remaining anonymous.

To Abram the God of the Hebrews said, "Get out of you own country, out of your fathers' house, to the land that I will show you." There was something about the old environment that posed a threat to the rising star of Abram.

To become the patriarch of a great culture and religion some things in his life had to change. The first of those was environment.

I don't think the change was comfortable for him, I think it was a lonely route he took; 'The Road Less Travelled' as Robert Frost would say.

None of his fore-bearers ever did anything like that. He probably was fiercely criticized by his clan but what did Henry David Thoreau say many years later?

"If a man does not keep pace with his companions, perhaps it is because he hears a different drummer. Let him step to the music which he hears, however measured and far away."

God wanted Abraham in his own land, where he could be influenced by him and none other.

THERE-FONTEIN

One of my favourite teachers of the Bible, the late John Osteen wrote a book called, "A Place Called There". The book is based on the story of the prophet Elijah. After he had threatened to impose climatic sanctions - the absence of rain for years - to King Ahab.

The voice of God distinctly said to Elijah, 'Go away and hide by the brook Cherith' and he said, 'I have commanded the ravens to feed you THERE'. There as in, There-fontein.

In South Africa we would call this place Daarfontein, and this name would be used by people who say they hate Afrikaans. In his expositions he says, this place called THERE, is the perfect place to be, geographically, mentally and spiritually.

This is the environment of your inspiration and growth.

THERE, in Daarfontein there is no lack and no lack-lustre existence, because when you are THERE, you hear his voice and when you hear his voice your paths become paths of pleasantness and all your ways are peace.

THERE your potential is exposed and maximized. Though you often find yourself walking in the valley of the shadow of death you fear no evil.

During the days of slavery in America, there were two factions in the black liberation movement. One of the factions advocated for going back to Africa.

The other said we are Americans as much as all other Americans and we demand our rights as equals right here. We know from history that the 'Back to Africa' faction did not have success of any note. Whether or not America was right or not as an environment for growth, is immaterial.

No matter how hard and weird, the universe is on purpose, and all people that are in America, South Africa, Europe or any other place for that matter are not sociological accidents. The earth is the Lord's and the fullness thereof.

We have allocated ourselves pieces of real estate on earth but two people decide who lives where at any given time. You and God. If you don't like where God placed you.

Don't apologise, vote with your feet.

All we know is that Americans of African descent have made their mark on that soil in all fields of endeavour. Contrary to other erroneous views, they have not only dominated the boxing arena, entertainment, baseball, athletics and basketball. They are counted in economics, diplomacy, government, medical science, technology and all fields of innovation.

I would like to say I am *Ramalapan, Limpopoan* or South African but in truth I am none of that, I am an extraterrestrial being touring the earth with a mission to change the way the world and the way its people thinks about themselves, their God and why He placed them here at this point in time.

Therefore I am not fixed to an environment and I will not let the place where my umbilical cord fell choose where I spend the rest of my earthly life. I could not choose my landing but I sure can choose my ending.

RADICAL CHANGE OF ENVIRONMENT- MIGRATION.

What happened to good old migration, that power of movement that shifts people from environments that inhibit them? I believe people should rather be in places that exhibit them. The earth is an exhibition platform. The earth is the Lord's and the fullness thereof.

Whatever happened to the decisive force of migration. I sometimes think it's a crime to the God of all space to be born in one place, grow up in the same, be educated in the local school, marry a local girl, raise your family and pursue a career in the same place and later be buried in the local cemetery. Most people whose lives follow that vicious pattern leave behind them a biography like that of the legendary Solomon Grunday.

Solomon Grunday... Born on Monday...
Christened on Tuesday... Married on Wednesday...
Taken ill on Thursday... Worse on Friday
Died on Saturday... Buried on Sunday,
And that was the end of Solomon Grunday.

A *Pedi* saying goes, '*Lesogana le le sa etego le nyala kgaetsedi.*' - Loosely translated as, 'A young man who does not travel will marry his younger sister.'

Hillbillies marry or sleep with their younger sisters and give birth to morons. I don't know whether you know the difference between stupid and moron.

Stupid is offended when you call him stupid. A moron just doesn't get it. He just smiles like Mona Lisa at the same words.

One of the major differences between human beings and plants is that most plants are rooted to the ground as a matter of necessity and have very limited movement. That is for their own good.

Amazingly there are a lot of humans who seem to think they owe it to God to gravitate around the areas where they were born. The truth is, plants do well when they are rooted to one specific spot on earth, and humans don't.

You say a rolling stone gathers no *moss* - NOT ME, the other moss; and you can't roll without moving. You imply by so saying that moss, is important to gather so a stagnant stone would gather moss.

Why should you gather moss?

I am Moss and I don't want to be gathered.

I want to be scattered and free, as in free at last, free at last.

When the Group Areas Act was annulled in the RSA, there were black people who criticised the black people who moved to formally white suburbs. Later, the same critics moved to those areas but the prices had now gone so high they could only afford the smallest of houses having left their huge rural mansions behind.

If an environment does not suit you, it doesn't matter what the reasons might be, migrate. For those who are xenophobic, tough! We all come from somewhere and we are here because it was the last comfortable place our fore-bearers found.

If I was born in Rwanda I would probably have to decide whether I was going to be able to change the place or the place was going to change me. Since I believe in changing things, if the answer was negative I would probably move to South Africa and there be called a *kwerekwere*.

Life is too short to become a child soldier when you could be something better and fashion yourself into higher forms - even if it means being called a *kwerekwere*.

Jesus was raised in Egypt. So it means that even though he was the son of God a threat held on his life. Moses had to spend part of his life in Median, Africa again.

Joseph was a foreigner in Egypt but later became prime minister there. His birth and his calling were at loggerheads. He was born elsewhere but his star was to shine elsewhere.

He saved even the people from the place where he was born.

He was constantly seeking environments that would best groom the singular seed of himself.

"Death is more universal than life, everyone dies but not everyone lives."
— *Albie Sachs*

I would like to say I am *Ramalapan*, *Limpopoan* or South African but in truth I am none of that, I am an extra-terrestrial being touring the earth with a mission to change the way the world and its people think about themselves, their God and why He placed them here at this point in time.

Therefore I am not fixed to an environment and I will not let the place where my umbilical cord fell choose where I spent the rest of my earthly life. I could not choose my landing but I sure can choose my ending.

FOUR

ABANDONING YOUR TALENTS IN PURSUIT OF MAKING A LIVING

The day you were born nature had already provided two breasts filled with the tastiest most nutritious liquid that could ever be manufactured.

That simply tells you that making a living was long provided for.

It is making a life that will require effort from you.

There is nothing wrong with making a living, but that's not why anybody appeared on earth for. You surely didn't come here to earth just to eat and reproduce and be safe. That is perhaps the mission of the lower species, and believe me, I might even be wrong about that.

The animal and the plant kingdoms might even have uses beyond what humans assign to them. We might be making a grave mistake when we think we are the only things alive.

We think the sun is but an object.

How can a mere object keep the whole earth, the fauna and the flora, even the egotistical homosapien alive? The sun might be a god in her own right, and she might deserve her place among the living, even the life-giving. Think about the stars, the moon and the donkey and their possible heroic missions.

What comes to mind is the donkey that gave a speech in the Old Testament of the Bible, the ravens that fed the prophet Elijah, the dog that snatched a man's piece of meat so the man chased it and missed the lift going down the mine. The mine collapsed and everybody except the man whose meat was snatched died.

So in our naiveté, let us say birds are making a living, lions are making a living and donkeys are making a living. Making a living entails putting bread on the table under sufficient shelter and security.

It was Christ who said these words, "Therefore I say unto you, take no thought for your life, what ye shall eat, or what ye shall drink, nor yet for your body, what ye shall put on. Is not the life more than meat and the body more than raiment? Behold the fowls of the air; for they sow not, neither do they reap, nor gather into barns... Consider the lilies of the field, how they grow, they toil not, and neither do they spin."

He is saying, making a living is so low that even the fauna and the flora shun it in pursuit of being. I will admit though that one has to be at the final stage of being Grown-up — which is spirit, to be able to live at the level Christ is talking about.

Building a life is a much nobler pursuit. It comes out of understanding that you came to this world with a heroic mission and an overwhelming purpose, and that everything is secondary to that.

The best form of a show of such commitment and clarity of purpose is seen in people who pursue celibate lives in deference to their heroic missions.

People like Jesus Christ notwithstanding Dan Brown's allegations, the Apostle Paul, and recently guys like John Howard Brown. Of course it is not required that you stay celibate to prove your commitment to your heroic mission because often part of that could be linked with you having to be the conduit of the universe giving birth to its own missionaries and heroes, as the Virgin Mary gave us the Christ; as Elizabeth Mashamaite gave us Moss and as your beloved mother, and father of course, before I am accused of sexism, gave us you - 'You Incorporated'.

In pursuing your purpose, which is the reason why nature must have you or why God, Whoever He is to you, would have you here, you are going to meet a couple of formidable challenges. Chief among them is society - people. People close to you, people around you and people everywhere.

I believe if it is really true that we are going to come before the judgment throne of God one day, the most common excuse why people did not live up to His expectations is going to be — people.

By the Way I am more for the accounting throne than the judgment throne lingo. I am talking about giving a final report of your life. I think it will be done individually.

The whole idea of a long queue of the dead young and old before God has earthly origins. For this I apologise to the Apostle John, author of the book, The Revelation of John. As I said before, the Bible was not faxed from heaven. We like to queue so much that we think God is going to make us queue. I hate queues and my heaven must have none of that.

Every time you see a long queue it represents ineffectiveness and bad customer service. I think when you die heaven deals with you immediately. I am boasting good customer service and computer systems that would make Microsoft look both micro and real soft.

God is too alive and dynamic to put people in spiritual refrigerators waiting for a day of reckoning. Back to excuses, I believe most of the excuses would be phrased, 'My mother, said, my father wouldn't, my colleagues advised, my pastor recommended, and it was the wife you gave me', would be the classical male excuse.

The wife would say like the classical Garden of Eden broad, 'It was the snake'. Have you gone to church lately and heard how Satan is being blamed literally for everything that goes wrong.

It's pathetic.

It's about time people take on responsibility for their lives and failures. Leave Satan alone.

To hell with him anyway.

Own up and the sooner you do the sooner you will change your life for the better.

If you want to empty what is on the inside of you, I have one little piece of advice. You must learn to be independent of the good or bad opinion of others.

Abraham Maslow called it self-actualization.

If you are going to ever care about what people are going to say to you or about you I say, this world is not for you because in this world as I speak there are over 10 billion lips waiting to say something mean about you.

Deal with it.

HEAVEN IS A SCARY PLACE

Earlier in 2006 I gave a talk at my church in Tshwane (back then those that claim to know history called it Pretoria), entitled, "Heaven Is a Scary Place".

I thought it was a better platform for me to share my thoughts on the matter in a book. So when I found this blank space in this book I decided I would slot the speech right there.

> Most people believe that when they die they are going to walk down the red carpet and meet Jesus, or Buddha or Bahaiulah or anybody with a name that is not safe to give to your son.
>
> I say: No red carpet. No Jesus. No Buddha. No Bahaiulah.
>
> I say you are going to be received by a welcoming committee.

This committee will be made up of former earthlings who lived and operated within your talent fraternity.

People with almost similar gifting although their heroic missions would have been as different per individual as were their fingerprints. In other words, if you are a musician you would be welcomed by a huge committee, a cloud of witness of former earthly musicians.

The successful ones of course.

I don't know what heaven would do with the ones with buckets full of excuses.

In my imaginings the music welcoming committee is chaired by King David, who wrote and performed such inspired music that those who decided to put together the holy script could not but snug his book right there at the center.

This he did being king. Most kings have no time but for running their kingdoms and winning wars, be they physical or ideological. Being king was his career — a politician, but music, poetry and prophecy were his heroic missions.

Being a king was making a living - but being maestro and writing, and performing music and poetry of biblical proportions and magnitude – was making a life.

What a complete specimen of man he was.

Upon your entry into heaven's gate King David would sing your introductions in tones and strings of harp that would be pleasing to all within hearing of his composition.

Enter you, either head bowed or head held high in triumph. (By the way, this book is an intervention written to see that the latter becomes your posture on that fateful day, your day of pre-judgment.)

At this stage God is not even involved, he is still busy facilitating the comforting of your mourning family and doing 'a billion other things.

NOT THAT FAST, YOU ARE NOT OFF THE HOOK

I was thinking the other day of my first book.

It is a great book but it was not a successful project. By that I mean it did not land in enough hands. It did not fulfill its purpose, did not cause a revolution or a paradigm shift in our society as much as it was meant to.

I shifted my thoughts from that book to 'Ten Stupid Things Young People Say and Do'. My thoughts here were positive. I was self-congratulatory even in my musings.

I thought — finally, a successful project.

Then I heard a still voice saying, 'Just because you wrote the book does not mean you are off the hook'.

I heard myself asking, *Kganthe*, is there a hook. "Yes, there is a hook," continued the voice. "You are as responsible for marketing the book as you were for producing it. Which mother gives birth to a child and leaves it to fend for itself?

So, in accounting for what you have done with your talents you are going to have to take this whole lot from the initiation stage of the projects to the handing over".

So, because I wrote a book does not make me a great achiever.

To complete the mission I must still make it a point that the book lands in as many hands as possible. Artists who died poor and made millions postmortem are not to be adulated. I pity them no matter how great they had been. Yes they might have left a legacy, and for that I honour them. Let's try to finish what we start while we are still here. It's possible.

Let me tell you the story of my first book. When the thousands of copies of the first edition were delivered to my doorstep, I decided to use every method of distribution I could get my hands on. I did not even have a formal book launch.

Most bookshops rejected the book because of the many reasons they give when they don't want to do business with you. Bookshops?

Some people are just used to saying no they don't even know why they are saying 'NO'. I took my book, "Ten Stupid Things Young People Say and Do", to a bookshop in October 2006 and their buyer said that they were busy with Christmas purchases and that my book was not Christmas material.

What the hell is that?

What kind of book is Christmas material?

Jingle Balls by Santa Claus?

Deep inside the words welling in a bubble were, 'I will be back. I want to see what their excuse would be after Christmas.' I am not going to let absentminded people like that stop me.'

So the bulk of the copies of my first book were sold during my seminars and conferences. So I used what I call the traditional methods of publishing. One of these traditional methods was a guy from Venda. He took a huge bundle of my books and went to sell them there.

I was very popular in that area in those days, so the books sold like the apples from the Garden of Eden.

Then after he had collected the money, I reckon he took the trip back to Polokwane, but somewhere in Makhado he just saw this car he couldn't resist. He was one of those guys who could resist anything but temptation.

He took that money that belonged to me and bought himself a car. But because he was not astute at the art of wheel and gear the self-same day he drove his or our little car into a tree.

So we can safely conclude, that the launch of my first book was on a tree in Venda.

NOW LET'S GO BACK TO RECEPTION AT HEAVEN'S GATE

After King David's introductory song, the heavenly host of former earthlings will resonate in one voice or hymn: 'Show us what you did with your talent'.

"I sang in church, and there was a guy at Universal Studios that did not like me.

'Ahaa?' "Lucky Dube stole my demo."

'Ahaa?' "I wasn'tpretty enough, the scouts were prejudicial to pretty faces."

'Ahaa?' "The guy at Idols was mean."

'Ahaa?'

After all excuses, Ray Charles will say, 'But I was blind as a bat'. Beethoven would say, 'I composed some of my best music while I was deaf'.

Then they will put on a plasma screen and there they will display the budget. What was budgeted for project you? Five billion dollars. Time span to run — 5000 years at least. How long did it run? Fifty years — meaning it expired the day you left your body.

How much of the budget was utilized? Fifty thousand Zimbabwean dollars. They will also show you all of the resources on earth that were earmarked for your use. All the people who would serve as your angels in this incarnation and all the angels assigned to Project You.

You say is there anything like that? I say there is.

I say to you that the cure for every ailment in the world is right here in the universe. The solution to every problem in this world is right here in this world. The provision for every need be it financial and otherwise is right here in the world.

You are the field of all possibilities and infinite creativity.

You are pure knowledge, infinite silence, perfect balance, invincibility, simplicity and bliss.

You are the eternal possibility, the immeasurable potential of all that was, is and will be. You are a god in embryo just waiting to manifest. The sad thing is if you discover all this in scary heaven, before a tribunal of people who were outstanding on earth because they were privy to these gems and you weren't, then you will have discovered these gems too late. When l say it's stupid to say it's too late I am only talking about the time before this serious tribunal.

A POWERPOINT PRESENTATION?

Yes, a PowerPoint presentation of:

Projected. Actual. And Variance, will be flashed before you and everyone present and you will have to explain the variance.

While you explain the variance, all musicians who ever lived will be there except of course for Bob Marley. Because ole' Bob will be in the garden trying to dry the leaves of the tree in the middle of the garden; so he could get high just one more time.

Then they'll ask you, 'Do you still want to see Jesus?'

You'd be saying, 'Jee-Who. Neh'.

I just want to go chill with Bob. Where is Bob at?'

SCRIBES' WELCOMING COMMITTEE

This one would be chaired by the one and only king of Poets, William Shakespeare. "So thou *Mosseth Mashamaiteth*, how *pleadeth* thou before this noble *lekgotla*'?"

"Eh eh Mr Shake... A teacher and author at the back who used to finish student's sentences says, '... Speare'!

"Oh Mr Shake Speare I must say, I am sorry. I tried but then there was this guy in Venda, and a tree and a car. Besides you guys if it's you, who snapped me before I could really give it one dying shot, if I had just lived for five more years I would have done greater."

Then John Keats will say but I lived for only twenty six years, and Percy Bysshe Shelley will say, make that twenty nine. Shakespeare himself will say, 'I was around earth for only 52 years, and OK. *Matsepe* would say, 'Make it 40 for me'.

So folks give me hell anytime, burning flesh, I like a good piece of meat on the fire, flames – I have a fire place in my house. But accounting for years of sitting on God's stuff on the inside of you might be the greatest scare of the hereafter.

Let me tell you a story I heard. It's about a beggar who had been sitting by the road-side for way over thirty years begging.

One day a stranger walked by.

The beggar stretched forth his begging container, 'Spare some change, please' he mumbled as he was used to.

"I have no change to give you," said the stranger With a rather soft voice. Then he asked with renewed interest, "What's that you are sitting on?"

"Nothing", replied the beggar. "Just an old box. I've been sitting on it for as long as I can remember. Many years it's been since I have fallen on my misfortune."

"Have you ever looked inside," asked the stranger'?

"No," said the beggar, "What's the point? There's nothing in there. It's an empty box."

"Have a look inside," insisted the stranger.

The beggar managed to ply open the lid.

With astonishment, disbelief and elation, he saw that the box was filled with gold.

At this point of your reading consider me to be that stranger asking nothing more of you than for you to look inside.

Of course you might not consider yourself a beggar, but if all you are doing in this life is to make a living, you might as well be the beggar because you are focusing your life's energies on stuff that Jesus said birds, animals and even the green inhabitants of this world regards as mundane.

I didn't say you should abandon making a living, I said do not abandon your talents and your gifting for making a living.

Learn multi-tasking from your body.

As I was writing this book, my body was doing a million other things. Pumping blood, digesting food, fighting viruses, building up the immune system, thinking, storing fats, but at the same time I was Writing a book and thinking of you.

The billions of cells in our body have been out-thinking us for years without end.

They can multi-task because they are more in touch with divinity than us who are plagued by the barrier of the incessantly thinking mind.

Even though the ability to think is one of man's greatest distinguishing features, it is the ability not to think that would elevate us above the earth plane.

If we can learn the art of silencing the mind we would take on the subliminal intelligence and brilliance that our cells display on an unending cycle of eternity.

"The individual has always had to struggle to keep from being overwhelmed by the tribe. If you try it, you will be lonely often, and sometimes frightened. Bur no price is too high to pay for the privilege of own in g yourself."
- *Friedrich Nietzsche*

The day you were born nature had already provided two breasts filled with the tastiest most nutritious liquid that could ever be manufactured.

That simply tells you that making a living was long provided for. It is making a life that will require effort from you.

FIVE

WHAT ARE PEOPLE GOING TO SAY?

Let's admit, a lot of people you know live under the constant fear of criticism and the constant need to be approved by others. I heard somebody call it *approval-addiction*. If before you do anything you think about what people would say or what people would say if you fail you have a huge problem.

There are only two times in your life that people will talk about if your name should ever come up - when you do something and when you do nothing. But, mostly people talk about the man or woman who is moving and rising, the person who is doing something.

They will call you all sorts of things just to strike up a conversation.

The weather is out of fashion these days, it is the weatherman who is being talked about - The man who tells people to put on warm clothes because it's going to be cold. If it turns out cold nobody is going to say anything about the weatherman, only the weather.

If by some stroke of fate it becomes warm they are going to fry the weatherman in the sun. Should the weatherman stop his job, no.

Like the horoscopes and fortune-teller who predicts through the constellation of the planets what is to be, the weatherman should wake up the next morning with no shame on his face, and face the day with yet another prediction. Otherwise he is the weatherman not the weather boy.

My question to you today is, 'Are you the weatherman or are you the weather boy?' Decide, and to hell with people.

Talking about boys and men, a friend of mine brought a young gentleman to me who had travelled more than three hundred kilometers to look for a '*directly sold*' suit from him.

My friend sells Italian suits directly to the public.

He said to me, 'Meet my friend, he is a man of God'.

We greeted, and his friend, without any solicitation from me began telling me about his impending marriage. He was a twenty four year old full-time pastor who was getting married to a seventeen year old. After many exchanges of thoughts, I asked, "Don't you think she is a little too young to get married?"

I knew I had no business asking that question but l did.

He said, "Not at all, in fact she is even more mature than I am."

I imagined she probably had a bosom like that of Dolly Patton and a bottom that would make Sarah Bartman turn in her grave - physically matured, because I couldn't figure out how a seventeen year old girl could be more mature than a twenty four year old minister.

But then again full time pastors with pitifully small churches that hardly take thirty minutes out of the pastor's day are usually unemployed stupids who don't want to face reality.

I saw one of those praying for the unemployed to get jobs and I muttered, "Shouldn't charity begin at home if nowhere else?"

I said to this friend of a friend, "That your seventeen year old wife-to-be is more mature than yourself says more about you than it says about her."

He looked at me with glistening eyes and said, "Amen my brother!" So he didn't get it. I told my friend later that his wedding-suit-client was not a man of God, but a boy of God.

Just because you stand before a pulpit doesn't make you a man or a woman of God. Just because you teach in a classroom doesn't make you mature.

Just because Johnny and Paula call you daddy or mommy does not make you a Grown-up. It is only when we audit your life that such a conclusion could be arrived at. A creature that puts on silk is a worm but a creature that puts on pants is not necessarily a man, it could very easily be a mannequin.

More than anything else being a Grown-up means being able to stand up on your own two feet and look at the world squarely in its dubious eyes and say, 'Find somebody who gives a fart'.

To be a man you must be self-reliant.

Henry David Thoreau said: "Who so would be a man must be a non-conformist".

Abraham Lincoln said: "I do the best I know how, the very best I can, and I mean to keep on doing it to the end. If the end brings me out all right, what is said against me will not amount to anything. If the end brings me out all wrong, an angel swearing I was right would make no difference."

If you want to empty what is on the inside of you, I have one little piece of advice. You must learn to be independent of the good or bad opinion of others.

If you are going to ever care about what people are going to say to you or about you, I say you will never amount to much in this life. Most of the great people I know have an 'I don't give a damn' attitude towards the babbling masses'.

A good example of a man who was independent of the good or bad opinions of others was a man known by the name of H.L. Mencken.

Mencken was a twentieth century journalist, satirist, social critic and freethinker known as the "Sage of Baltimore." Others called him the "American Nietzsche." Mencken is arguably one of the most influential American writers of the early 20th century. He was greatly criticised for his controversial and pungent lines. At the height of his illustrious career he published the following letter in one of his columns.

> To anybody who might send something critical to me.
> This is my response.
>
> I'm sitting here in the smallest room in my house.
> (I am sure everybody knows what that room is).
> With your letter of criticism before me.
> Soon, it will be behind me.
>
> H.L. Mencken

I am sure there is a way and an attitude to tell people off without necessarily making them look stupid. But that was Mencken's style. I'm sure you are saying, 'Look who's talking?'

DO YOU KNOW THIS MAN?

I would like to ask you a question but I also would like you to be very honest with me. Here is the question. Do you know of any guy called Eliab Jesse?

Next question, in the history of civilization is there a guy you ever read of or heard of with the name Eliab Jesse? I didn't think so.

Let me narrow it down. If you are a reader of the Holy Bible do you know of a guy called Eliab? Negative.

Eliab is a biblical non-figure who is quoted in the Book of I Samuel Chapter 17:28. I would like to go verbatim on him before you judge me or him.

When David went to the war zone to give his brothers food, he sensed the fear in the warriors of Saul, something he was not personally acquainted with.

He also observed a man with an enormous head and a body to go with it, who was bellowing threats and insults at the nation of Israel.

He asked who the man was and they gave him the name and the background. Then he wanted to know why everybody was listening to his insults to Israel and to God and doing nothing about it.

Silence, except for the sounds of chewing gum.

Then he asked the dude next to him what would happen to the man who would kill the uncircumcised bastard.

How David knew he was uncircumcised beats me.

Perhaps Goliath after expressing himself in great bellows and threats, would parch his throat and ask for water. The more water he would drink the more his bladder would bulge and then he would take more leaks than the average Philistine. And maybe David saw him pee before he heard his boastings and bellows. I think he saw him pee through his rather abundant foreskin, I wouldn't know for sure.

The people of Israel had been waiting with abated breath for a man of the caliber of David and just about when he showed up people were beginning to say their say, and people very close to him for that matter.

People, people, people. Who is, 'People?'

My friend Mokgadi Mathonzi gave an amazing oration the other day about 'People,' the big P.

She went, "I surfed the Internet, called Home Affairs and finders of missing people trying to find out who this guy called *'People'* is.

In fact at the same time I was doing this, she continued, heaven was sending down one being to earth to go and get some background on this person called *'People'*. Reason being that 98% of all people who passed on and achieved below target and failed to deliver on their heroic mandates, said they had simply been afraid of what '*People*' would say.

After much research heaven also hit a blank.

Then she went on to tell a story about frogs that were trapped in a rather deep and narrow hole. There was no food down there and they knew that sooner or later they would starve.

They all started to climb up the narrow incline, but as they were going up '*People*' began to criticize. "Who do they think they are?" "Ain't no way they are ever going to make it out of that rat hole."

Yeah, I've seen this happen before, frogs trying to get out of a deep narrow hole like that. They died.

Another story — 'I read a book that said categorically that only vermin can navigate themselves out of such a trap.'

An educated one — 'According to statistics, ninety-nine, point nine, nine, nine, nine, nine, nine percent of such attempts are doomed to failure. The remaining zero point one percent that makes it to the top just hits the ground and dies instantly out of exhaustion.'

Of course nobody will tell you that, ninety nine, point nine, nine, nine percent of all statistics are wrong - including this one. Having listened to *People*, the frogs gave up and resigned themselves to the effortless death of starvation.

But wait a minute.

One frog kept trying for days without end until on the tenth day she made it to the top and out of the hole.

When news broke out that one frog made it the media flocked to the scene - videos and cameras flashed as they bombarded the frog-let with questions of how she made it through.

She kept blinking at the flashing of lights but said nothing.

They discovered that she was actually deaf.

Moral of the story? You figure it out. In this world young or Grown-up you've got to choose your own path and follow it.

Sometimes you will have to adjust things and change course but be brave enough to do so without asking anybody for permission.

You don't owe anybody an explanation, you are Grown-up aren't you. A friend of mine wrote this beautiful poem and I think you should reflect on it and draw some strength from it.

The Path Of Life

Silence nurtured me in the belly of peace
There in a woman's womb orders were given to my effect
In birth I cracked silence with my first cry
All that cry to my mother's joy
Souls in my youth presented me with their paths,

Or so they thought but none resembled mine,
For my soul knew no satisfaction
The urge to search embedded in my soul gave me no rest
With zeal and zest l followed and imitated
The paths of great men to my frustration

Dancing to the tune of no identity I nearly gave myself up
In despair! Wondered how silence in her beauty
Of quietness could send me to a world of no name,

For I feared she would summon me to my grave
Before I found my path and conquered my pursuit
But now beinga Grown-up not in years but in being,

Have I realised thatsilence ushered me into this world
Not to follow a path but to create my own

- Abram M. LELAKA

Early in 2006 I gave a speech at my church titled, 'To Hell with Satan.' I was *gatvol* with how Christians had made such a big deal of Satan.

If you listened to the opening and closing prayers at churches (themselves totally unnecessary) and also listened to individuals in group prayer, the name of Satan features with a frequency second to God, even to none.

If you were not a Christian at all hearing these things, you would surely want to meet this *grootman* called Satan.

But second to Satan as the big deal, is the big P. When the question hits you, 'To P or not to P', I advise not to Pee. I think I should go back to speak and this time rephrase my message — 'Never mind Satan, to hell with people.'

It was with great pain when Oscar Wilde observed, "Most people are other *People*. Their thoughts are someone else's opinions, their lives are a mimicry, their passions a quotation."

"The secret to success is failure; the secret to fast success is fast failure; the secret to big success is... big failure. It is failure, not success that makes the world go around. Because failure typically means that someone has stretched beyond the comfort zone and tried something new... and screwed it up and learnt something valuable along the way."
- *Tom Peters*

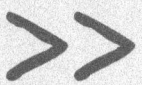

More than anything else being a Grown-up means being able to stand up on your own two feet and look the world squarely in its dubious eyes and say, 'find somebody who gives a fart'.

SIX

THE FEAR FAILURE

The fear of failure ensnares most of the Grown-up people of the world. Young people are typically not slaves of this phenomenon. I read a lot of biographies and even though I am captivated by the heroics of the great people that inspire epic biographies, I am not so blinded that I cannot see together with their heroics, their failures too.

I think to be a great success one has to fail a whole lot more than the average people do to become average.

We can therefore conclude that - average failing will only lead to average success, and great failing will lead to great success. Of course this depends on maintaining an attitude that says, 'It's not over until I sing'. Let's leave the fat lady out of this because she might just be *your mamma*.

While at this, don't provoke my *'Your mamma jokes'*. 'Your mamma is so fat, they named you *Surprise*'. Want more? Pas op!

Bottom line is, it is stupid to sit on your butt doing nothing, fearing to fail and scared of what people would say about you if you fail.

To be successful one must self-actualize which also means to be independent of the good or bad opinions of others. You must be not only bigger than criticism but bigger even than compliments. People who want praise too much have not self-actualized.

Understand me, everybody can do with compliments once in a while, but when it becomes your diet as in fish, chips, coleslaw and compliments - with cream!

Then you've got a problem.

It is Grown-up to allow yourself room for adjustment, which means the same thing as room for failure. I am not talking about being negative here. I am one of the most optimistic guys you'll ever meet, and an incurable one at that.

If you bludgeon my optimism with disappointment, optimism ten times stronger arises in me. What I am talking about is the ability to rise up when you've fallen instead of beating yourself up like it was the end of it all.

THE WILLIE SNYMAN LICENSE

I have had great mentors in business. The first was George Lundsberg who was my manager at Sanlam. Then there was Solly Matjekane who was the top dog at the then Southern Life. Solly was the first guy I personally knew who knew how to say 'Happy Birthday' with a German car. Now that is what I call eloquence!

Then came Willie Snyman in Pretoria. When he hired me at Sanlam Head Office, I was the second black guy to be hired at that level in the company and the youngest of any race. South Africa was transforming and the integration experiment was on course.

Willie said to me; 'Moss, I want you to know that here you are allowed to make all the mistakes you can, don't be shy. I realise that you are a very creative person and I don't want to interfere with how you do things'. That spurred me on to greater success. Even though I was hired as a training consultant my freedom to fail spurred me on to a greater role. I soon found myself doing management consulting, conducting strategic planning sessions for line management and filling other management consulting roles.

I had the greatest gift on earth.

The freedom to err without shame.

Oh how I wish people could give themselves the Willie Snyman license. When there is no fear of failure people operate with greater liberty and creativity. In the presence of fear people stifle every other energy to uphold the status quo and hold on to the minimum standard. Every work place and project environment needs a Willie Snyman.

It was Mahatma Gandhi who said, 'Freedom is not worth having if it does not include the freedom to make mistakes.'

A few years ago, the Economist published a feature on the success secrets of Silicon Valley. Topping the magazine list of traits that distinguish the Valley was the Pursuit of risk.

That is looking failure straight in the eye saying, 'Do your damnest but I am still here, we'll just see who will endure. "It's Last Man Standing" kind of mentality.

Fear of failure means pursuing the risk-free lifestyle of job security, not rocking the boat, and adopting the 'yes-boss attitude' in life.

Fear of failure excludes you from success just like fear of death excludes you from living. In combat battle the soldiers who survive are the fearless.

Shaka Zulu used to kill any soldier who came back with wounds on their back. That's why he was the great general he was. You can't win a war with cowards no matter how superior your arsenal, and you can't fulfill your heroic mission if you are a coward.

With failure there is always embarrassment but I'll tell you, there is no need to be embarrassed at failure because effectively about eighty percent of the people of the world are failures, but you don't see them embarrassed.

They usually don't think they are failures. They think the guy who is attempting great things and floundering, is the failure. They never fall because they walk along life's solemn main with baby steps, such slow-paced effort there is no possibility of falling.

You see them celebrate their mediocre lives with a *braai* and you pity the cow whose brisket they are munching and what it does to the cow's self-esteem to know the quality of teeth that is ripping into its tissues.

Postmortem that is.

If you have learnt to celebrate failure as a revelation towards future success, you are free. A friend of mine once cashed out his huge pension funds and bought offices to open a brokerage.

He went broke and lost most of what he had.

I met with him at the beginning of a new business venture and I asked him what had happened. 'I lost all my money but I consider it to be school fees. I had to pay that much to learn valuable lessons. But I am still here and a hell of a lot smarter'.

That, right there, is the only Grown-up attitude towards failure I know. Failure must be embraced as the flip side of the success coin.

It was Michael Schrage, the innovation guru who said, "Those who are willing to invest in and test unproven ideas, based on a hunch or a gut feeling are likely to find their noses bloodied routinely; but by the very act of entering the fray with vigour they increase the odds dramatically of joining the small sect of True World Beaters who shape tomorrow's extraordinary contours."

I enjoyed the moving picture Coach Carter, starring Samuel L. Jackson who is arguably one of the best actors of our day. In the movie the Mexican boy Lopez who lives a double life of a tough street-wise boy and whimpering kid, is confronted with the rest of the boys by the coach's hard question — 'What is your greatest fear?'

Only after he triumphs over his fears because of the inspiration and support of Coach Carter, and after he observes fatal failure and realises that his chosen path will only lead to disaster, he stands up and gives a soliloquy of his greatest fears.

His greatest fears are verbalised in the eternal words famously quoted and embellished by Nelson Mandela from Marianne Williamson's book — A Return to Love:

"Our deepest fear is not that we are inadequate."
"Our deepest fear is that we are powerful beyond measure."
"It is our light, not our darkness that most frightens us."
"Your playing small does not serve the world. There is nothing enlightened about shrinking so that other people won't feel insecure around you."
"We were all meant to shine as children do."
"It's not just in some of us, it's in everyone."
"As we let our light shine we unconsciously give other people permission to do the same. As we are liberated from our own fear our presence automatically liberates others."

LONG FACES

In their fear of failure Grown-ups live sulky lives. They live and look like people on a lemon and lime diet. They seem all retired from the practice of joy, a necessary and good practice.

As a growing child I always wondered why my friends and I were always so happy while our role models, the Grown-ups were so sulky. They were proprietors of faces longer than those of Turfontein race horses and I wondered why.

I found out that the difference lay in failure and success. As children when we failed we simply tried again. Just after learning to stand up we tried walking, it was a rigorous effort. One day just take your time and observe a toddler trying to stand for the first time and what happens when he falls down in failure.

They giggle in amusement.

That's perhaps the most beautiful sight on earth to me.

I would choose to watch a baby learning to stand or walk than to go and see the Seven Wonders of the World.

Even as the little one giggles a couple of seconds later it tries again; and that's going to be again and again and again, until the act is perfected. No long faces.

I hate long faces!

On a daily basis I talk to many people I meet and joke with them - trying to cheer them up, and make them happier, but some people don't get it at all. I have seen sworn proprietors of long faces protecting their territories fiercely as if saying — LONG FACE ESTATE — trespassers will be persecuted!

At the very end of being Grown-up, is old age.

Lots of people at this age do not have their teeth. Of course they lose other things too, things which we shouldn't talk about lest we reach that age we feel bad about what we had said while spurred by the seeming infinity and almightiness of youth.

When you grow older, you get yourself a new dental formula because when you pass that toll gate - OLD AGE PLAZA, you pay with your teeth. So my advice to you is, before you pay with your teeth show them around just a bit. Smile until you look beautiful. If you are beautiful already, smile until everyone around you feels beautiful.

I hate Grown-ups when they hide their teeth.

Give me toothy Grown-ups any day and I am cool as a cucumber.

When I was a pastor in my early twenties I had a lot of children in my church. I remember when one of them was asked at school what he wanted to be when he grew up.

He said he wanted to be Pastor Moss.

That's what they called me then.

One day I went to this little one's crèche for some business. It appears that the little politician had already campaigned for me. It was break time when I arrived and somehow they all left their food and came to touch me.

I was in a car and they were more than a hundred.

They swarmed the car and touched it saying, '*Bhuti Moss, Bhuti Moss*'. The teachers tried to stop them so they could go back to class, but in vain. School was delayed for about twenty minutes. I never had so much love from so many young minds fill with passion.

I felt like Michael Jackson after a splendid performance being loved by a crowd. Perhaps it's not Orlando Pirates who are the happy people (May the Lord raise they spirits)

These free to fail people are the truly happy people of the world.

They take on life one effort at a time; one day at a time and they do not lump yesterday, today and tomorrow in one sad day of regret, uncertainty and seeming doom.

They live in the eternal now and therefore live life to the fullest. Christ, speaking to a bunch of Grown-ups said, "Unless you convert and become like little children you will never see the kingdom of heaven."

I was on Radio 2000 on Ms Cookie Mokaba's show and she asked me a question, "Moss, what would your lesson be to a young man who had never had a father on, "How to become a good father and not be abusive to women?"

My answered was, I'd say to him, "Take a trip back to when you were a little boy. What did you want out of a father or even a husband for your mother? Now tap into that purity of wish and capture your aspirations then, and then you would not but become a good father and great husband.

See your mother in your wife and you will do the right thing" In other words, to be a good Grown-up you've got to be a child. I know this sounds like a paradox wrapped in a mystery, but it's true.

My friend Fortune Nithoro once asked his four year old nephew what he wanted to be when he grew up.

He stood up and spoke in a highly modulated voice, little chest heaved up, "When I grow up, *ke batla ho ba grootman.*" Meaning, when I grow up, I want to be a big man. Everybody listening laughed at that but if I remember well, that's all I wanted to be when I grew up.

To be a Grown-up so that I could do all the things Grown-ups said we couldn't do but they themselves did.

I wanted to smoke until I looked like a goods train.

I wanted to drink like a fish and be drunk because Grown-ups looked so cool when they were drunk. In fact most of them looked happy only when they were soused. I wanted to come back home at twelve midnight. No questions asked.

I simply wanted to live without rules, and as a child there were just too many rules, and if you added to that the Ten Commandments, in fact eleven - the eleventh being thou shalt not speak back - it was too bad.

It was as if as Grown-ups were bent on making the happy people's lives miserable. Then I didn't know that when I become a Grown-up, I would still need to follow some basic rules to become a happy person.

I had to be Grown-up to realise that rules would still need to be adhered to.

THE EARTH DOES KINDA SUCK

Newton gave us gravity.

Believe me, this won't make God jealous.

Before Newton the wisdom of the day was, the earth sucks.

Truth is, it does *kinda* suck, but you don't really have to participate in the sucking. Newton also said it, what goes up must come down.

It is important when you are rising either up the corporate ladder or up any ladder for that matter, that you must observe gravity.

There is no need to derive self-importance out of success and treat people like they were less than you. On the flip side of the fear of failure is the inability to handle your success - which is just as bad as the fear of failure.

Rudyard Kipling, English novelist and poet captures everything I said in this chapter, "Being independent of the good or bad opinions of others, and not falling into the snare of self-importance and yielding to the egotistic mind."

He captures all that and more in just one poem - IF.

The poem IF, starts with IF and ends up with — you'll be a man my son — meaning you'll be a true Grown-up. He goes:

IF you can keep your head when all about you
Are losing theirs and blaming it on you;

If you can trust yourself when all men doubt you,
But make allowance for their doubting too:

If you can wait and not be tired by waiting,
Or, being lied about, don't deal in lies,
Or being hated don't give way to hating,
And yet don't look too good, nor talk too wise;

If you can dream — and not make dreams your master;
If you can think— and not make thoughts your aim,
If you can meet Triumph and Disaster

And treat those two impostors just the same:
If you can bear to hear the truth you've spoken
Twisted by knaves to make a trap for fools,
Or watch the things you gave your life to, broken,
And stoop and build 'em up with worn-out tools;

If you can make one heap of all your winnings
And risk it on one turn of pitch-and —toss,
And lose, and start again at your beginnings,
And never breathe a word about your loss:

If you can force your heart and nerve and sinew
To serve your turn long after they are gone,
And so hold on when there is nothing in you

Except the Will which says to them: "Hold on!"
If you can talk with crowds and keep your virtue,
Or walk with Kings — nor lose the common touch,

If neither foes nor loving friends can hurt you,
If all men count with you, but none too much:
If you can fill the unforgiving minute
With sixty seconds 'wOrth of distance run,

Yours is the Earth and everything that's in it,
And — which is more — you'll be a Man, my son!

RUDYARD KIPLING (1865-1936)

FAILURE GIVES BIRTH TO PAIN AND PAIN HAS ITS USES

Let me at this stage strip failure naked — FAILURE is pain. In the following paragraphs the word failure is going to be used interchangeably with the word pain because that is the essence of failure. Therefore people who fear failure are, in fact afraid of the pain that goes with it.

Is failure your enemy or your friend? The answer is yes and no. It depends on where you accord the impostor failure - a place in the calendar of your life. If you say to failure, 'You are the Omega, the end, the writer of the final episode of my life', then failure becomes a fatal enemy. But if you say to failure, 'Failure, you are the alpha, the beginning, even the transition, and the writer of chapter one in the turn-around history of my life'.

Then failure becomes your friend.

Legend has it that one day two young Greek students came to Jesus with a quiz formulated to make even the greatest of wits to flounder.

The fame of Jesus as the '*sakyas munus*' of the age had reached Athens where heads were swelling with knowledge and philosophy.

One of the two philosophers-in-the-making showed him his hand, closed it into a fist and said,

"Rabbi, what do I have in my hand?"

"A bird," answered Jesus.

The boys were impressed.

How did he know? Takes more than wisdom.

Perhaps the rumours about him were not exaggerations.

"Now tell us, wise man, is the bird dead or alive?"

They had intended that if he said it was alive he would squeeze it dead, and if he said that it was dead he would open his hand and let if fly away.

The bird was so small it wouldn't take a feat to accomplish that. "Young man", answered Jesus, "the answer is in you hand."

Whether the bird is dead or alive depends on you.

The young Greeks, like the Pharisees and the Sadducees were beaten. In the same breath, whether failure will become your friend or foe depends on you.

There is a level of failure that men often reach that forces them to make quality decisions that awakens their slumbering genius. A level of failure that makes them stand on the two feet of their souls and say, "Bring it on, give me your best shot".

It is also important for one to perceive failure for what it truly is. A teacher - true, and a negative one at that, but a highly effective one.

If people perceived failure for what it is -

Bankruptcies would not give birth to business has-beens.

Divorces would not give place to other divorces but to successful marriages and more - to marriage counsellors.

Failure in any field would not give birth to failures but to successful people.

Just don't let failure strike you the terminal blow. Let it rather be a wakeup call — a rude awakening if you please.

THE REAL FORCE BEHIND HISTORY

Behind great heroes of the epics of old and of the modern day, there lie scars hidden deep within. Behind the breath taking stories of the history makers of our age and ages past, there lies this great impostor- Failure.

Moses the prince was transformed into Moses the slave when he observed the pain of the Israeli slaves, and Moses the slave was transformed into Moses the fugitive when desperation forced him to take the law into his own hands.

Moses the fugitive was turned into Moses the deliverer when the melodious music of Median was drowned by the cries of slaves back in Egypt – the transformation of a mortal life into a life immortal.

A transformation that gave the world and history perhaps its greatest leader of all times.

Napoleon was a second class citizen in France as a Corsican. His schooling was in institutions where his fellow students did not hesitate to remind him of his citizenship status. The pain was unbearable. It pushed him towards the re-definition of the citizenship of all Corsicans in France when he became the Emperor of France.

Of all things that have inspired the world into peacefulness among many speculations, I believe the foremost is failure. Never mind diplomacy and the increasing quality of international statesmanship. Never mind the rise into world power of countries that espouse democratic principles. Failure has been the foremost.

The ravages of the two world wars, especially the last, the loss of lives, the drawing back of civilization. World intelligence and growth would be at science-fiction levels if we had not incurred losses and suffered drawbacks through the Second World War.

Who knows the potential of the people who died during the war?

What dreams did they have? What visions had they seen?

The Nazi era, that beginning of a return to the dark ages did more harm than could ever be measured. Books that promoted non-Aryan ideas were thrown into heaps and publicly burned.

Scientists who had worked in inspired teams in Institutes of Science were separated and isolated, with the Jewish lot running away for their lives or being massacred. Great brains were employed by small brains for the destruction of the world instead of progress (some willingly and some unwillingly).

Considering the influence of the people of Jewish descent on science, physics and commerce at that time in history, how much do you think we have incurred in the loss of six million of them?

Need we say anything about the Hiroshima and Nagasaki waste?

This excludes assets like fixed property that were annihilated by the $E = mc^2$ formula among others. A formula birthed by the mind of a pacifist genius who meant no harm to the world. Unfinished projects by lives that were terminated prematurely. Young and old businesses that perished, and sibling ideas that were aborted and not given a chance to bud by the war.

The Second World War and its wastages and ravages drummed sense into over 3 billion heads, and sent a message that said, last warning - a repetition of this and you are all ashes - it's Armageddon!

Although the peace has not been a perfect one, it has been peace where the world of nations is concerned. That failure created pain and pain is not without use.

IF I COULD JUST HAVE...

Most people live their lives bending over their regrets. The things that happened in your life and the things that you did cannot be changed. They will remain done things.

Dealing with failure does not have anything to do with bending over and trying to redress the past. You can condemn yourself over your past or you can ask for forgiveness.

Forgive yourself and move on.

Four things never return, said a wise man; 'four things come not back - the spoken word, the sped arrow, the past, the neglected opportunity'.

The Apostle Paul says, "...This one thing I do, forgetting those things which are behind, and reaching unto those things which are before."

The Apostle Paul's things behind included the murder of innocent people - a life of religious intolerance and fanaticism. If he dwelt on those, he would have become nothing close to what he became.

Bottom line, no matter who you are and what you've done, and how old you are, your life is not behind you.

It's all ahead of you. I have heard people tell young people, 'Your life is all ahead of you'. I am saying it to everybody — to you!

A guy came to me and told me that his social life was messed up. I asked, 'Why?'

He said, 'Well, I am a divorcee.'

I asked him why he was allowing an event like divorce to become a defining attribute of his existence.

When you say I am divorced you are mentioning an event in your life. When you say I am a divorcee, you are naming yourself after the event. I said to him, 'Call yourself a used husband if you will or, a pre-owned or pre-loved man but not a divorcee'.

Like everybody else I failed in a couple of endeavours, but that does not make me a failure. I have lost some battles but I am not a loser. I have dropped a few points in my sojourn but I am not a drop-out. I got broke big time at some time but I am not poor.

I failed once in marriage but I am not a divorcee.

I am God's understudy, an apprentice to The Great I Am.

Since I have such an enormous figure to look up to and emulate, I often fall short, but I am not a short-circuit in the distribution of divine energy on this green earth and galactica.

The poet and astronomer and the world's most famous tent-maker Omar Khayyam wrote:

The Moving Finger writes; and having writ,
Moves on: nor all thy Piety nor Wit
Shall lure it back to cancel half a Line,
Nor all the Tears wash out a Word of it.

Leave the past where it belongs. In the past. Behind you.

Give no second glance to your failures, take your lessons with you and move right on. Lot's wife turned into a pillar of salt by looking back. Your turning back could transform you into something worse, like ice cream.

Wayne W. Dyer says that one of life's greatest illusions is the belief that the past is responsible for the current conditions of our lives.

All great men and women, stripped of the mythology that often builds around them, are common clay like all of us, and they go through failure even more than the commonest of us for them to climb the summits they have.

Let's therefore, when we ascribe greatness to them, remember that to climb up to the summits they have, they have had to fall countless times more than those of us who elected to lead our lives in the valleys of mediocrity.

The light bulb is a product of about almost ten thousand failures.

Disney World is a product of about seven bankruptcies.

The match-stick was a failed attempt at creating gold.

Need I say more?

"Ambition like fire lies latent in all nature. And subtle are the naked desires of all of nature. The goat dies and transforms into an oak. The oak desires to become coal. The coal's ambition is to become a diamond. The diamond would love to become love pure and true. And as love he caresses gently a maiden's love finger. A token of undying affection, to forever linger. With all of the fragrances that makes up the best of nature.

  - *Moss Mashamaite*

Like everybody else I failed in a couple of endeavours, but that does not make me a failure.

I have lost some battles but I am not a loser. I have dropped a few points in my sojourn but I am not a drop-out.

I got broke big time at some time but I am not poor. I failed once in marriage but I am not a divorcee.

I am God's understudy, an apprentice to The Great I Am. Since I have such an enormous figure to look up to and emulate, I often fall short but I am not a short-circuit in the distribution of divine energy on this green earth and galactica.

SEVEN

ABANDONING THE AMBITIONS OF YOUR YOUTH

What did you want to become when you were young? And what did you become? Or, what became of you? If I may ask, what happened? Sitting down looking at yourself through your rear-view mirror do you have any regrets? Why are you doing this to yourself?

What bitter waters washed down the force of your ambition?

What circumstance decided that you take the path that you are now on? Too many questions? Sorry but I feel obliged to ask.

The Oxford Dictionary defines ambition as an ardent desire for distinction, an overmastering desire; aspiration to be or to do an object of such desire.

The Latin word is *'ambitionem'* or *'ambire.'* To be ambitious is to be strongly desirous, as if there is some kind of fire burning in your bones.

Many Grown-ups look at ambition as some quality much less than modest. Some people even regard it as evil. An ambitious man is therefore a man to shun, somebody to stay away from. If you ask me, ambition is a form of inspiration that has no consideration for fact or reason and consideration for fact or reason has left multitudes in the valley of despair.

Going back to Carl Jung's stages of adult development, I must admit that ambition is primarily an attribute belonging to 'The Warrior' stage of development. Yet this does not reduce it to that intermediate stage of development, because no matter how subtle, ambition is a divine attribute. It runs through all stages of adult growth but assumes different forms at every stage.

In the Bible the story of Joseph teaches us the divine power of dreams, but also reckless ambition. I hope I am not using the word reckless, recklessly.

The story of Jacob his father, teaches us the divine power of ambition, even cunning and shrewdness which themselves look like dark forces. But are they really? Wasn't it Christ who said, "... to be as wise as a serpent yet humble as a dove?" Shrewd without being harmful to others, business sharp - profit minded without being a cheat.

Let me parade a couple of people known and recorded in history as having been ambitious. Alexander The Great wanted to conquer the whole world of his day, and in his own way he did. Today his spirit lives in you and me. We still want to conquer the world but not with a sword. I might have elected to do so with the pen, you might have chosen a blunter instrument like a cello or a guitar. But fact remains fact, we are ambitious. I am writing and you are reading. That is romance. I may be on top during this round but we can change positions any time, especially when you play the cello.

You picked up this book because you want more.

That is ambition.

Napoleon Bonaparte wanted to be the Emperor of France while he was not even a true French man according to the citizenship definition of his day. He was a Corsican from Ajailon and was looked upon as a second class citizen, if a citizen at all. As history will attest, it all happened as according to the ambitions of his great heart.

You and I, and Napoleon have something in common.

We would like to redefine our citizenship in the world. We may not go about it the same way he did. Since our ways are of peace there will be no Waterloo on our path. Even though there is, unlike Bonaparte - we will arise and walk, for we have also made peace with failure.

The fact that the red blood of ambition often courses through the veins of warriors and sometimes evil men, has made the good people of this world suspicious of this great force that leads to personal accomplishment. In my studies on this subject I was shocked to discover that ninety percent and more of what is written on the subject is negative.

It seems as if mortal religious man sees ambition as nothing other than the force that led to the demise of one of God's arch-angels and turned him into the ugliest of menaces. That is for those who subscribe to the popular biblical interpretation of the rise and fall of Lucifer.

In my opinion, Lucifer - as narrated in the Bible was brought down by his desire to become what he could never be - God.

Ambition is desiring not what you can't be, do, or have, but what you can be, do or have. We can aspire to become gods not God - to become his understudies, not him.

He lives most who regards himself an extra-terrestrial being, a god in their own right. This according to some people is too ambitious and vain but I don't think so. You can be a worm or a mammal and as one so-called intellectual said, 'a speck of dust with delusions of grandeur' (man that is).

I elect to be God's apprentice, a god in embryo, daily transforming myself into my full potentiality.

The world's attitude towards ambition is expressed in William Shakespeare's Brutus referring to Julius Caesar, saying; "As he was valiant, I honour him; but, as he was ambitious, I slew him."

Are we going to be the brutal Brutuses of this world and slay every whim of ambition in our hearts? The reason I have pushed the lesson on ambition to the Grown-ups book is because ambition seems to be despised as people grow older, and it is the demise or death of this life-force, that destroys the chances of most Grown-ups.

One thing that waters down a Grown-up into a grown-down is the loosening of the screws of ambition by Father Time. I've had breakfast with the younger generation and I have dined with the older, but the younger are more intriguing because they have unreasonable ambitions by the standards of their elders.

I met a young man who said his dream was to harness the electric power of lightning into a usable form of energy; and one who wanted to annihilate a whole religious sect that was constituted by millions of people. Grown-ups would just be wanting to pay up their bills. 'If I could just pay off my Edgars account I would be okay.' Sad, isn't it?

'WHEN I GROW UP I WANT TO BECOME THE PRESIDENT OF THE UNITED STATES OF AMERICA'

This was said by a primary school child in Uganda.

I spoke to a Grade 2 child from Uganda, asked him my favourite question for young ones. What do you want to be when you grow up?

He said President of the United States of America. Even I was shocked - but also delighted.

Shocked-delight we must call it. I discovered the little one was tired of his mother's repeated attempts to obtain a visa for entry into the U.S.A. being rejected.

He had decided that if he became President of the U.S. of A, his mother's destiny would be in his own hands. I'll cut convention into shreds.

The divine forces of the universe (I hesitate to say God, because in your mind he will have a great white beard — Bin-Laden equivalent and a big rod like that of Moses with punitive powers) speaks through ambition. You can quote me on that.

Unlike humans, the divine force does not shun ambition. The divine force does not look at ambition as evil. Ambition, like money, is purely amoral. It takes on the morals of its subject. Therefore there are evil ambitions and good ambitions, just as there are good desires and evil desires.

There is one particular biblical narrative that I find intriguing.

It is the story of a man named Isaac who was blessed with twins. The first born was called Esau, a mighty man, a hunter of game. The second born was Jacob, a domestic man, as home based as their mother.

Jacob was not satisfied with the fact that he was the second born. The reason being that the royal sceptre of Chaldean patriarchs only landed in the hands of the first born.

What made it worse was the story he had heard from his mother about his grandpa Abraham. That the old man used to be a buddy of God, and used to almost speak face to face with Him. That during one of those days of fellowship God promised to make him a great nation. So all this meant to him that Esau would be the carrier of the promise, not him.

The young boy saw two destinies before him: Obscurity as second born and prominence as the first born. He could imagine the riches, the power and the glory that went with the position. It was attractive.

Intention is itself a force that has within it, the seed for its own fulfillment. Its ways are past finding out and they manifest in the form of seeming coincidences.

As one man aptly said of coincidence — it is God's own way of remaining anonymous.

One sunny summer day, Esau, heir designate to the 'throne' of Isaac, came back home famished. He checked the kitchen, the pantry, the pans, and the pots for something to eat. Nothing!

Esau was forced to do something that he was averse to - beg.

He approached Jacob and asked him for something to eat. He showed him his pottage, very appetizing. Esau tried all the tricks in the book to get it, begged, pleaded and persuaded and even threatened his brother but to no avail.

"But since you insist,"

The younger brother later repented, "I will give you my pottage, but there is a price attached. There is nothing for free, ain't it so big brother?" Said Jacob repeating Esau's favourite words for effect.

"Okay what's your price?" Asked an unpleasant and not too impressed man.

"Well, since you are asking, my condition is that I become your elder brother, the first born of my father." said Jacob unashamedly.

"Are you crazy? That is an absolute absurdity." Sorry then big brother, your request is as absurd as my price, have a great day."

Esau made a quick run through the slow computer of his mind trying to figure it out. "This is insane - I will always be your big brother, the first born of our father. Birth has dictated it so and who can alter such. This boy should be kidding. What difference would it make?"

Even while he was pondering upon this, the hunger was slaying him dizzy, for he was a man mighty around the table and weak to hunger.

"Okay, you got me," he said. "You are the elder brother and I am the second born, right?"

He spoke it with unbelieving nonchalance while his hairy hand was extending towards the seductive bowl.

"Not so fast younger brother," resisted Jacob. "You must first sign these papers here. In triplicate."

Esau could care less. What difference would three pieces of paper do to change reality? A piece of paper could not change history, he thought.

He didn't realise that what may not change reality may still change destiny - the reality of tomorrow. He then signed without reading and ate his food with great appetite. He ate his birth right for a dessert while Jacob stood watching with self-satisfaction.

When blessing time arrived, Jacob cheated his blind father, and it was okay. He had bought the inheritance for a bargain price of one bowl of pottage. In today's terms it would be like buying the whole of Microsoft with R3500 worth of bunny chow.

Jacob knew when to go for the jugular. From then henceforth, God who could have become the God of Abraham, Isaac and Esau, became known in all of history of religion as, the God of Abraham, Isaac and Jacob.

I'd venture to say God rejected Esau because he lacked ambition.

I also believe what made David to stand up to Goliath was 50% faith and 50% ambition. More than once he asked what the King would do for the man who would slay the giant.

That question was definitely not asked by the faith element of his nerve but by the ambition element. The God of the Israelites, observing that flame of ambition in the young lad overlooked his brothers and the genetic successor to the throne, and anointed David King.

Joseph's ambition of becoming a Great One that would be worshiped by his brothers and parents, alienated him from his brothers and earned him the suspicion of his parents but endeared him to the Power that guides the tides.

Though his life story takes us through pits, prisons and slavery, the fire of his ambition could not stop burning until its smoke had become the incense of the royal court of the great Pharaoh.

Think about it. A boy in rural surroundings which in contemporary circumstances would be equivalent to what we call the *bundus*, speaking no English and literally living in what would be no less than the armpit of the world in total obscurity. This boy says, "When I grow up I want to become the President of the US of A."

What do you say to such a boy?

You say, "Stupid! Who bewitched you?"

Let me tell you little ugly thing, why don't you take your head to the auction and relieve your shoulders of unnecessary weight. I'll give you ten reasons and more why what you are thinking is not only impossible but ridiculous too.

Let me tell you why it will never happen. Not now, not ever. Not in ten life times, not in a zillion years.

One - you are not American, two, you don't even understand their language, blah, blah, blah!.

The end of the story proves that Joseph had been right.

You can dream without limits and still see your dreams take material form however lofty and unreasonable they seem. His inspiration was genuinely from that great power that stirs the winds and rules the tides.

What Joseph's society would unflinchingly call crazy ambition was God's inspiration.

Bishop Wright had two sons. He was a very intelligent and eloquent man. One day in one of his celebrated orations he categorically declared that man would never be able to fly. Simply because he was never meant to. Flying was the prerogative of birds and not men.

His sons, Orville and Wilbur did not think so. Their ambition was to one day fly above the capability of eagles. This was raw, unadulterated ambition. It might not seem crazy today, but then, the word crazy would most definitely have been an understatement.

They became the first men to successfully take to the skies.

It was ambition that made interplanetary travel possible.

It was ambition that landed the first man on the moon.

It is ambition that has steered the human race from the Stone Age to the Computer Age.

This force that steers men and women is been controlled not by chance but by God himself. To have good ambition is therefore to hear from God.

It is to draw strength from the breast of the Almighty.

HOLD ON TO YOUR AMBITIONS AND LEAVE YOUR CHILDREN ALONE

I have seen so many parents trying to live out their earlier foiled ambitions through their children. It's wrong. 'I want my son to become a doctor,' is a common phrase these days.

Leave your son alone and pursue your own ambitions.

Get over yourself already.

You failed to become a doctor, your maths was just not enough, leave your son alone. I know a lot of miserable doctors who would have wanted to become something else. Ask your daughter or son what she wants to become, don't force her to become what you wanted to become and couldn't become. Your children are not here to correct your mistakes or to augment your shortcomings - they are here on divine mission of their own.

If you could understand a deeper Grown-up statement I would say to you that your children have really nothing to do with you.

At a higher level of being they are not even your children.

You were simply the conduit.

Yes you have the important job of raising them to be greats and you should, but remember that in their own right they are divine beings.

Furthering this debate, I can show you people who were not raised by their parents but still became who they were meant to be. Les Brown, the multi-millionaire world famous motivational speaker and author, was an adopted orphan and Wayne Dyer, author, motivational speaker and spiritual guide of many, grew up in a series of orphanages.

My mother died when I was three years old and my father? I don't know what happened to the cowboy. But we are all children of the universe and the divine force does guide our stars. Do not ever want to re-live your life through your children, they were created for other purposes, larger purposes than to spite your neighbours or show your village one or two things.

Another show of the abandonment of ambition is when parents start to surrogate their children. They want to live their failed lives through their children instead of still sticking to their dreams and ambitions.

They want to dump their lives on their children.

You are still here, and while you want to help your kids reach the summit consider that you may need help yourself. To be a single parent you must help your children and show them the way, but you cannot afford to neglect yourself like you were dead as a person and only alive as a parent.

"Like a pillar of light Man stood amidst the ruins of Babylon, Nineveh, Palmyra and Pompeii, and as he stood he sang the song of Immortality: Let the Earth take. That which is hers, For I, Man, have no ending."
 -*Kahlil Gibran*

You want to show anybody one or two things, do something – yourself.

Ambition is the core element of the universe. The dead log of wood yearns to become a rose or coal.

The coal's ambition is to become diamond; and diamond wants to find itself on the finger of a rose checked maiden.

EIGHT

WHEN I DIE

Have you ever listened to the 'When I die' trash that people share with you thinking it really matters and you are really listening? Here you are and as clearly as I can see there isn't much to your living and you want to interest me in a little story about what you would like when you die.

'When I die I want to be buried in a grave with my head facing east'. 'When I die I want to be buried putting on my favourite Giorgio Armani suit'.

'When I die I want to be cremated and my ashes spread in the Vaal River'.

When you die, my foot! Why don't you opt for living, why don't you rap, 'While I live'? Better still why don't you opt for never dying.

I will give you my opinion about eternal life.

Christ said that those who believe in him would not die but have eternal life. He did not say those who make a religion about me or those who idolize me, he said those who believe in me.

What then is this eternal life? What was he talking about?

The whole concept is rather confusing when you consider that man is an eternal soul. How do you promise an eternal being eternal life? How do you?

Christ must have been talking about something else.

He was saying all these to his disciples who were known to believe in him. So he was talking on a much higher dimension. He meant those who go beyond what is called, 'believing in Christ'. Those who really get the essence of what I am saying and what I represent.

Those, the true believers, would be buried in the ground, but their testimony, their essence will remain. We are talking about immortality here, immortality in a place known for transience and mortality, earth! Definitely he couldn't have been talking immortality in the hereafter because every being there is already immortal.

Where I stand it matters not whether your head faces east or west in your grave. It matters not whether the ashes of your cremation are spread in the Vaal or the Ganges. It matters not what the vicar says during your funeral. It matters not how long and poetic the eulogy. It matters not whether your family and friends cry themselves a river mourning your departure, what matters is how long your essence will remain after your burial. Will you leave anything eternal behind? Will everything about you expire the day of your burial?

As far as I am concerned, you can criticise Lebo Mathosa all you want, you can ridicule Brenda Fassie all your breath allows you to, you can even go about telling people how much weed O.K Matsepe smoked; and how much Samuel Taylor Coleridge was addicted to drugs, but what you can never achieve is erase those people's footprints on the sands of time. Eternal time, I might add.

It was the poet Rumi who said, "When you are dead, seek for your resting place not in the earth, but in the hearts of men."

Milton wrote a poem for Shakespeare.

In it he is reflecting on the legacy that Shakespeare left behind. (My interpretation) He is marveling about the enormity of his works and contribution. In great subtlety he argues that Shakespeare should not yearn even for a memorial tombstone, saying that he is actually too great for such, that his proud and worthy tombstone remains the works and the legacy he has left behind.

In his own words, "What needs my Shakespeare for his honoured bones, the labour of an age in piled stone? Dear son of memory, great heir of fame, what need'st thou such weak witness of thy name. Kings for such a tomb would wish to die."

Get me clear. I have got nothing against honourable funerals and tombstones. When I die I want to be buried decently and commensurate with my lifestyle and economic status. Your pauper's funeral might prove a point or two for me but I am only asking for consistency.

If I refuse for my toilet a single-ply toilet roll, do you think I would want to be encased in a tomato box at my burial?

Besides, I have a very good relationship with tomatoes and therefore I would not temper with their house. Those who advocate for cheap burials with tomato boxes for coffins have never really lost a loved one. Jesus was buried in a wealthy man's grave. There is a bit of shame when your father is buried in a tomato box, even if he himself was a potato or a grown-down, problem is, it could reflect on you.

To your father I say, if you can live your life up to eighty years of age and cannot afford to bury yourself you are pitiful.

Burying yourself is not even an option.

Leaving an inheritance for your children is a must.

I think anybody who dies and leaves their children in poverty having had the opportunity to cover their needs at least with life assurance; should go straight to hell whatever hell is, and wherever it is.

If for some reason they make it to heaven, they will appear before the Financial Provision Committee (FPC), and there they would have to account.

I think the FPC is chaired by Judas Iscariot. Christ forgave him, deal with it! He was a hell of an accountant too.

With countless Life Assurance companies around offering products and soliciting clients aggressively, you've got to be stupid to have nothing to leave behind.

I personally blame fathers every time I see a prostitute; but for most taxi men I blame mothers. But what I am talking about here is leaving an inheritance not only for your children's children but also for the whole world.

Leave your ideas, your music, your poetry, your industry, your efforts, your empire and your essence behind. Your body gone never to be seen again - prove to the world behind that you were more than the body that encased you, that 99 percent of you was spirit and therefore invisible. Let the invisible you be forever visible years after you have passed on.

I was raised as a Christian, mostly of evangelical persuasion and most of what we were taught is that when you die you must be ready to meet the Master, Jesus. Their angle was that you be found sinless, holy and pure. My problem is, having been a pastor myself for almost ten years I have never met a person who was either sinless (I have met *sin-less* chicken though, sorry; skinless) or holy or pure.

I have just met a lot of pathetic people beating themselves up for being human. I have seen sorry unhappy people who looked like they were on a lemon and lime diet in an attempt to look holy. I have therefore decided that when you die, to be ready to meet your maker you must have a final report of what you spent your life doing on earth that is worthwhile and that the people that remain behind would still be able to enjoy.

I think the final report would be like that of a General going to see his Commander in-Chief after the war is won. The Commander in-Chief will not focus on his scars or how dirty and bloody he looks - not even on the number of casualties, but on the results.

Am I saying people should not try to be good people, holy'?

No, I say give it a shot; but that's not why you are here. In the morning you give your children clean clothes when they go to school. When they come back you expect them to be in an acceptable condition. You don't expect them to be as clean as when they left, you expect them to come back with good grades.

You ask them what they learnt and ask them how they fared. You look at the dirt on their clothes and you throw everything in the washing machine and prepare new clothes for them for the next challenge.

Like the 'OMO' ad you say, 'This is not dirt, this is a gold medalist'. So, we evangelicals were made to emphasize coming back home as clean as when we left or else, instead of coming back home with the spoils of war; the medals. Wrong!

THE MYTH OF LONG LIFE

When I was a young pastor I used to preach the charismatic doctrine of long life. Now looking back I realise that I was preaching long life for the sake of it.

If we don't know what we are here for and are not even making an effort to discover that, what is the point of being around here, and that for a long many years?

Now I don't care about living long any more, I care about living much. If one really understands purpose and divine missions, and that the essence of our being here is to fulfill those missions, then the whole question of long life becomes totally irrelevant.

If your mission here was to discover the cure for Aids and give your remedy to the people and future generations, and you are able to accomplish that at the age of thirty five, and save the world from a pandemic, and you died after that - you would not have missed nothing.

All you might miss is the Nobel Prize.

A prize Jesus wouldn't have cared for. A prize George Bemard Shaw didn't care for.

Jesus' mission was accomplished at thirty three. Shakespeare died at fifty one. Did they need to live any longer really? Long life is emphasized by those who live like this earth is the final destination of man.

Man existed as a spirit before the earth was and will exist forever after. Our being on earth compared to our being is like a shooting star crossing the skies. It is dramatic and terribly short-lived. I say to you, 'Be a star, and a shooting one'.

The period of your dramatic life is totally irrelevant.

When we look at the biographies of men we don't really check how long they lived and how they died; but how much they lived.

I understand the desire to growing old to see your grandchildren but at a much higher level your children are not even really yours, they belong to the universe. You were the conduit and of course you are responsible to steer them towards their heroic missions.

In my teachings about long life I even taught that a believer should die in his sleep. There were nobler ways to die. Dying in a car accident or of disease was wrong. Now I know that there are a thousand and more ways to die and none of them is nobler than the other.

There are only noble ways to live.

In my narrow 'noble ways to die doctrine', I never asked myself why Jesus died naked on a cross and why Cicero was beheaded and his hands cut off — both to be displayed at the speaker's forum for six months until they stank and decomposed. I did not ask myself why Chris Hani and Martin Luther King and IF K died of bullet wounds.

What about Steve Biko and the Apostle Peter.

Is there really a noble way to die?

Today I will say that I would rather die like Steve Biko or Martin Luther King than die in my sleep, because there was nothing to really wake up to. I would rather die early having accomplished what they had accomplished than live as long as your grandpa has and have nothing to show for it.

There is no point in some people living long because all they do is to participate in consumption without contributing in production.

A repetition of many routine and stupid years.

Most of the people I have heard saying the damned words, 'when I die' had never spent a single day planning their lives. Ain't nothing wrong in planning your exit but shouldn't we be planning our entrance first. By your entrance I am not talking about your birth - that and its pleasures had nothing to do with you. Your entrance is the day you announce yourself on the world stage saying, 'I AM HERE', 'I am a soccer star', a musician, a writer or a teacher!

By your entrance I am talking about your debut.

Tokyo Sexwale entered the stage the day Chris Hani was assassinated. King David entered on the stage of Goliath and Rebecca Malope on the Shell Road to Fame Stage.

The universe keeps affording us such stages for our entrances and most of the time we are preoccupied with making a living and we ignore these moments.

I remember a friend of mine and I were offered an opportunity to write a vocational guidance book which had a great chance of being prescribed. We locked ourselves in the house for a week to produce the book.

When we were done, we decided we were not vocational guidance pro's. Both of us were good writers - educated and street smart. We left the book and went on to pursue a guy who had a doctorate in vocational guidance so he could partner with us.

He was illusive and busy with his own stuff. The time we spent pursuing him was enough to have us fail to meet the submission deadline. We had to kiss our entrance goodbye.

Imagine if we had produced a prescribed book - me at twenty eight and my friend at twenty six. It would have hastened our impact in the book market.

We lost that moment and every time I think about it I bleed.

But I have made up my mind that is not happening to me again.

WHEN I GET TO RETIRE

"I envy not in any moods,
The captive void of noble rage
The linnet born within the cage,
That never knew the summer woods:"
Alfred, Lord Tennyson

When I get to retire is a subtitle in this chapter because as far as I am concerned it means the same thing as "When I die." Great people don't retire, they expire. They die.

Why then should small people have the prerogative of retirement?

Nelson Mandela tried to retire but could he really.

The "Don't Call Me I Will Call You" speech was simply amusing. The next thing after that speech he was fiercely campaigning against Aids. The life-force in him is just too much for repose.

One of the most stupid things I've heard Grown-ups say is planning for retirement. There are a lot of business ideas that have been put on the when-I-retire shelf. There are books and music and poems that will be written, when I get to retire.

Firstly, who said you'll get to retire?

Secondly, why postpone passion to the passion-less period of your life. Who's going to look after my children and tell them '*verhale van menige avontuur*' while you'll be busy with your newly formed construction business.

If you were so passionate about business why didn't you do it when you had the strength? One of the most pathetic things I've seen in this world is people who didn't live their lives at all, trying to do it later in life.

I have seen a sixty year old man trying to start a soccer team for pensioners. They left soccer for education during their days, activities that could have been pursued concurrently any day by anybody able to walk and chew gum at the same time. Now at sixty, retired, he wants to start a soccer club. You talk about singing 'Bring back my yesterdays!' This time it was a choir on stage.

He found several idiots his age to buy into his idea.

They chased the ball around and coughed their lungs out, but they hardly ever got to it. They had fancy and energetic football nicknames too. The entrepreneurial soccer star himself was called Viagra and it was clear he needed Viagra just to kick the ball.

The goalkeeper was called Red Bull.

He was ruddy of face and as be-wrinkled as an old sheet.

Pitiful tired beings trying to live earlier dreams.

Saying, 'When I get to retire' is wrong because when you get to retire you tire.

When I was a young pastor I was told by some older pastor that it was good for me to have older people in my church. I asked why? He said, 'They add stability to the church'. I asked how? He said because they seldom change their minds.

Imagine trying to transform people who seldom change their minds? It would be a total waste of time. The whole idea of church is to have people who are prepared to change their minds and the way in which they live.

If I wanted to be a pastor I would want a church made up of people who believe they could change. People who still believe they could change their circumstances. People who still believe that 'now' is the time.

Three things the Apostle Paul said; "Love, Faith and Hope." Love has been over- emphasized, especially by musicians and shows such as 'All You Need Is Love'. I am saying, what about faith and hope. Where there is faith and hope there is material for greater possibilities.

Where there is hope and faith people jump out of bed to face life.

Give me people who jump out of bed any day no matter what their age and circumstances, believing they can change the world and I will give you heaven on earth.

The only thing we should postpone for retirement is retirement itself. Your life is today and it must be lived urgently, today.

"Life is a game, play it; Life is a challenge, Meet it; Life is an opportunity, Capture it."
– *Unknown*

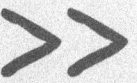

Where I stand it matters not whether your head faces east or west in your grave. It matters not whether the ashes of your cremation are spread in the Vaal or the Ganges.

It matters not what the vicar says during your funeral. It matters not how long and poetic the eulogy.

It matters not whether your family and friends cry themselves a river mourning your departure, what matters is how long your essence will remain after your burial.

Will you leave anything eternal behind? Will everything about you expire the day of your burial?

NINE

BLAR, BLAR, BLAR... WRITE YOUR OWN.

But before your do. Imagine...

"Not merely an absence of noise, Real silence begins when a reasonable being withdraws from the noise in order to find peace and order in his inner sanctuary."
– *Peter Minard*

...imagine

TEN

MIGRATING FROM THE WOMB OF SILENCE

When you have read chapter 9, you will know I am not a man of few words. My first temptation was to leave it blank as I have done in my previous book. But I hate predictability and routine. I hate routine so much that I often sleep in the different rooms of my house just so I do something different.

Of the words I write appears in chapter nine - 'Imagine' is the most important. You can fly on the wings of imagine. That's where I want to take you. Imagine if you were to fly ahead of the fiery chariot of your imaginings.

Imagine if you were allowed to live your life all over again?

What if I was to tell you that you can?

Imagine is the angel that grants you the grace to live again. Christ said to an old man that he could be born again. What is to be born again really? It is to start afresh as though your previous life had been erased, and the bad experiences with it buried, while the good experiences and lessons of that period remain.

Imagine if I told you there was a cure for stupidity. Imagine that I am saying to you right now, 'You are healed. Take up your bed and walk'.

Back in our school days, the child who let their imagination soar, the civil engineer who defied gravity and built castles in the air, was dealt severe punishment for not paying attention.

Paying attention to what, I ask?

Jan Van Riebeeck, the lizard and its cloaca'? They tried to kill that genius many years back but that same genius is now reading this book and undoing what has been done.

The journey of life begins with you crawling, toothless and basically helpless and it pretty much ends where it begins. It's a circle.

We started this journey with Carl Jung's four stages of adulthood development and we should end it on that note.

WHERE DO YOU PLACE YOURSELF ON THE LADDER OF GROWTH?

As you read now you are either an Athlete or a Warrior or a States-Person or a Spirit. These stages are not necessarily cast in concrete and they could easily blur into each other, and one person could move from one stage to another in split seconds. So basically here, your category becomes the stage where you spend most of your daily allocation of time.

It is important to be honest with yourself and begin working on changes towards the next level. There are things that you should do in order to move to the next level.

Before I even get there I must clarify that you can achieve great things from any stage, but always remember the wisdom of Emerson - "The height of the pinnacle is determined by the breadth of the base."

ETHNIC CLEANSING

Were we to place all your excuses in one basket, the most numerous of the items in the container would be - the great P - *People*.

One of your greatest obstacles if you want to be the 99% that you are mostly leaving out of your existence is *People* - the stranger you know nothing about but have delegated a great amount of influence to. So we begin this exercise by removing all the *People* who stifle your growth into the next level of being.

One of the most fascinating narratives from the Bible is that of the man who spent thirty eight years of his life lying next to the pool of Bethesda waiting to exhale. Jesus asks, "Would you want to be made whole?"

The man replies, "There is no man to throw me into the water."

In other words, I am what I am because of what people are not doing. Folk either blame people for what they are not doing or for what they are doing.

I heard a fifty something year old man saying about himself, 'I am just a poor orphan'. I thought, orphan at fifty something?

What does he want?

To suck his mother's breast again?

At fifty-five if you went to suck your mother's breast the best you would get is low nutrition skimmed milk. Imagine now, a fifty-five year old *malnutritioned* stupid orphan.

Oh shame Benoni, next door to Boksburg!

So if you are to move to the next level you are going to have to ruthlessly massacre the tribe that surrounds you and inhibits you.

I call this ethnic cleansing.

There are four worlds in your life. The physical, the social and the mental and then there is the other world, the spirit world.

So to get to the other world, the spirit world, you must transcend the physical, the social and then the mental. I will not waste time on the physical. It should suffice to say that you are not a body and the sooner you get out of that fixation the better.

The person we call Moss Mashamaite is just the garage where I park my real self. Look at it as a 'Rent A Moss' kind of arrangement. Now let us begin by killing the inhibiting crowd.

I divide people — the tribe into five types of insects. I chose insects because they are the most *'annoying others'* in our lives, that's why we call them pests.

I was young and now am old, but I have never seen anybody making pets out of pests. I have seen pet lions and pet elephants. Heck, even pet snakes but never a pet cockroach.

The pests that I think need to be taken care of, in the *Italian Mafia* style are - mosquitoes, the house fly, the bee, and the cockroach. Then there is the ant. A total different story on its own.

The Mosquito

I wrote a note to a friend the other day saying, the saddest thing about living alone is that when you get back home all the mosquitoes in the house are just too happy to see your ass, or is it cloaca?

It's not because they love you. The mother mosquito would be announcing as soon as she hears the garage door open.

"Beloved, dinner is served."

While they dine, the talkative one in the family will be on her cell phone calling a boyfriend. "Hey where are you at?"

"I am somewhere in Hercules, some big Afrikaner's house, they call it a *huis*. And where are you?"

"I am in Moss Mashamaite's house."

"THE Moss Mashamaite?"

"The one and only."

"How is his black ass?"

"Mmmrn, delicious!"

"I told you about black people!"

Mosquitoes want your blood, your energy, even your substance.

Most people leave themselves surrounded by homosapien mosquitoes they call friends. You must make a social audit and categorize the tribe that surrounds you. For mosquitoes I recommend Raid.

The one you plug on the wall. They will disappear out of your life.

When they leave, not only will you itch less, you will realise how much time you suddenly have with yourself, and with time there is more quietness and with quietness there is more reflection.

The House Fly

Whereas the mosquitoes come into your life in summer during the rainy season — a season of prosperity, the house fly is there all seasons.

What it does is, takes your crap to other people and then take other people's crap and brings it to you. There is no dull day with the house fly.

He is not interested in your energy or your money, he just wants to be with you and give you the stuff he has gathered about other people, hoping that you will complete the transaction by giving him some of your own and other people's stuff. The house fly is a busy body and the one way to get rid of him is by being too busy for him.

He is egotistical and cannot handle rejection.

As soon as he realises that you are not interested, he will walk out of your life and go out and tell people how bad you are and how proud you are. Don't worry about what he says about you, to hell with him.

He carries everybody's viruses and spreads them like a plague.

You will never grow when all you hear about other people is how bad or broke or loose they are. The only time the house fly tells you about another person's success is to make you feel bad. To actually say to you that compared with other people, you are not really doing so well.

For the house fly I recommend a pesticide with a bad smell, like the old Fast Kill.

Because his mouth is always open and he has a big nose anyway, he would be very intolerant to odours. When the house fly leaves, you will have more time but you will also know less about other people's intimate details.

You will therefore begin to love more because you know less. It's difficult to be nice to somebody on Sunday when somebody told you on Saturday that they hate you to bits. What you don't know can't hurt you.

The Bee

The bee likes sweet things. It either moves from flower to beautiful flower, from honey to sweeter honey and from pleasure to pleasure.

This is the party animal.

The guy or girl your spouse does not want around you. It is entertaining to hang around the bee but most of them do not amount to much, and their sting is infectious.

These people fit Sigmund Freud's view of man.

They spend the energy that successful people use to build industries, careers and homes, and blow it like a balloon on a Saturday night of Arabian pleasures. Most of their conversations are about the last awesome party they had.

They will always invite you, they will collect you too, and they don't like your spouse by the way. They don't mean to harm you, they are just lost souls campaigning for an accomplice.

They like you because you are funny or because your car is fancy or because you represent uppity or you are famous.

Mike Tyson had a swarm of bees around him when he was the meanest champion of the ring. He represented sugar, and bees like sugar. A couple of punches later, an ear bitten out of frustration, his entourage began to diminish while the bees went away looking for the next best thing.

How do you get rid of the bee? Simple. Every time he has got something going, tell him you had a prior engagement and mention boring things like church, library, the opera and mountain hiking, especially the library.

If he still doesn't go away, tell him you are experimenting on becoming a vegetarian and you are considering being baptized in the Zion Christian Church. He is gone.

So for this guy, no insecticides. Just holy tea and coffee and out of the window he goes.

The Cockroach

Some experts believe the roach to be a prehistoric creature.

I even heard somebody say if there was a nuclear holocaust roaches might be the only things that would survive.

The roach is that guy, that chick you have been trying to get rid of all your life.

He knows you don't like him and that he is not good for you, but he will cling like a limpet. This is a filthy creature that carries with it diseases that medical science has not even classified as yet. Even though he knows you do not want him around you he would be the first one to call you on your birthday.

One minute past twelve he will be singing happy birthday to you from his sinuses, some nasty melody or should I say malady that makes you want to puke but you still have to be polite. I have analyzed the tribe and insects, I cannot tell you exactly what the roach wants out of you.

In his own perverted way the roach thinks he loves you. He is Jesus Christ's Judas Iscariot, Moses' Dathan and Julius Caesar's Brutus.

He actually hates you and would destroy you if he could.

He is with you because he wants to see everything you do.

He is competing against you.

Anybody around you who is competing against you is dangerous. This one is beyond pesticides. Holy tea and holy coffee? He would drink it with you. How to get rid of him?

This is the only time I am ever going to tell you to get rude.

Tell him you do not need him in your life and say it strongly. When the cockroach disappears from your life it would be like the weight of the whole world is off your shoulders. You will have more than anything else, peace; and you need peace to get to the next level.

The ant

The ant has been in the construction business for millennia. I have never found an ant just chilling. If they are not building a multiple story structure, they are gathering stuff.

Not much to say, not being led or driven from behind, just self-motivated.

These are the kind of people you need in your life.

They are driven by purpose and their positive energy is infectious.

They have a keen interest in life and if they realise you are doing something better they would humbly request you to teach them and they would be just as keen to teach you something if you feel so inclined.

Remember they do actually party and recreate but they have not made that a lifestyle. These are industrious people who believe that they are here to change things and build something out of their lives. If you are lucky to find yourself surrounded by such you are on your way up.

MENTAL CLEANSING

My business brief - "Surround yourself with people who are better than you are, be ruthless when it's necessary." - Steve Booysen, CEO - ABSA

Once you have cleared the social environment a ruthless exercise is needed. You will suddenly be left with more time and are surrounded by people who would recommend to you a book instead of a beer. I don't think there is anything wrong with beer, I am just saying these new people in your life would be saying things like, have you read Sun Tzu's The Art of War or Deepak Chopra's The Book of Secrets,' instead of have you tasted the latest brew by Brewbarri?

People go to retreats on mountains to get mental cleansing. Some fast and stay away from food trying to find themselves or their God.

A couple of hungry days later they wake up to the realization that God was never in their stomachs in the first place.

Only the mind is the meeting or contact point between the world of the spirit and the physical world and it is in cleansing the mind that one can cross over from wherever you are, Athlete, Warrior, and States-Person to Spirit.

Remember the path is not necessarily linear.

Quantum leaps are also within the realm of possibility.

Mental cleansing is going to involve the following concepts - meditation, imagination, visualisation, synchronicity and primarily engaging in the act of silence.

I have read a lot of books on these concepts and I have experienced them myself but I will tell you that they are such subliminal concepts there is no actual method of either practicing or teaching them.

So I am going to follow my inspiration and just hope that when I get to the other side you are there with me.

SILENCE — THE GATEWAY TO THE NEXT LEVEL OF BEING

Perhaps the greatest blunder you ever made was to leave your mother's womb. Because there in that darkness, silence reigned supreme and creation continued unhindered. Then you were ushered into a world of noise, and for most, creation ceased.

Could it be that you died the day you were born?

From noise pollution, that is?

Is the world inhabited primarily by stillborn babies?

It was the wilderness that gave birth to Moses, for there in the silence of the fields bushes do burn. David was a shepherd and the silence of the woods plus the *silence of the lambs* gave birth to a King, a philosopher, a prophet and a musician.

Nelson Mandela's twenty seven years of isolation, as scandalous as it was, that was the womb that created 'The Madiba'.

Henry David Thoreau used to take long hermetic walks, and Emerson says about him, "...the longer his walks, the longer his lines". He wrote some of the most powerful poetry and prose that changed the way America and the world thought about itself.

Silence is the boiler-room of creation, the very womb. I have taken my time to write this book, said a lot of things, read and wrote poetry in the process, studied books by madmen and geniuses only to say one thing to you. You need to find yourself moments of silence daily in your life.

You say I don't know how to meditate.

I say who said anything about meditation?

I am talking about waiting upon the Lord or waiting in silence.

Yes, the chatter in your mind will begin, the Edgar's Account bill, your boss, your nagging wife, your stupid husband, sex and then more sex — they will all script themselves on the screen of your mind.

There are two ways to remove them and none of them is resistance. The first one is to let them play themselves away and give no attention to them until they vanish on their own, and they will.

Do not be impatient.

Imagine it's a cold winter and you are sitting around a burning wood fire. You are adding nothing to it, no more wood no more fuel of any kind. It doesn't matter how strong initially but if you are not fueling it, eventually it will die.

All you have to do is to camp silently around it.

When it finally extinguishes itself then a cold wind will sweep across you. The flames represent the chatter and the cold wind that sweeps across your body represents the breezes of silence when chatter gives way.

As your blabbering thoughts vanish they will give way to a sterile place between here and THERE and at this place your body and soul will begin to heave with sensation like a breeze on your most inner self, now concentrate on the sensation and play along.

Before you think about it you will find yourself in a place of such ecstasy and peace.

As you get used to it you will switch in and out of it.

Some days you will do better, some days worse.

But practice will perfect it.

The second way to deal with the chatter is with a mantra.

A mantra is an incantation - an instrument of thought. In South Africa most people are used to *toyi-toying* mantras that political activists used to work up their anger.

The purpose of the mantra is to focus your mind on the mantra rather than on the chatter. It gives the chatter no platform to express itself, in other words no air-time. Since the mantra is rhythmic and repetitive, sooner or later the mind will regard it as sterile silence and then the mantra has destroyed its own self.

Then you get to that place of silence and drop the mantra.

In essence I have taken you to the very door of silence.

While you are there you are on your own, it's a path you will have to explore. Those who fear that they would meet filthy spirits there should be admonished by the words of none other than Christ who said, "Ask, and it shall be given you. Seek and ye shall find. Knock, and it shall be opened unto you. For everyone that *asketh receiveth* and he that *seeketh findeth*. And to him that *knocketh* it shall be opened. Or what man is there of you, whom if his son asks for bread, will he give him a stone? Or if he asks a fish, will he give him a serpent? If ye then, being evil, know how to give good gifts unto your children, how much more shall your Father which is in heaven give good gifts to them that ask him?"

CHRISTIAN SCEPTICISM

People of Christian persuasion are very suspicious of meditation that sounds eastern. I say it's stupid suspicion. Mahatma Gandhi single-handedly brought the great British Empire tumbling down by using non-violence — a principle he had learnt from Jesus.

The 'Turning the other cheek' doctrine is not just a Christian doctrine, it is a spiritual weapon. He was smart enough that even though he was a Hindu he borrowed wisdom from Christianity.

If Christians are too stupid to do the same they shouldn't say I didn't tell them.

Moses, the finding patriarch of organised Judaism leaned Management Science from an African Priest - Jethro of Median. Judaism borrowed the wisdom of Africa and became a major force of its time. Now if Christianity must go to the next level, Christians ought to learn essentials like meditation.

Then they should be humble enough to ask, 'Who is the best in the field of meditation?'

Then they should learn.

The scripture in Isaiah that says, 'They that wait upon the Lord shall renew their strength, they shall mount up with wings as eagles. They shall walk and not faint', is not talking about waiting for prayers to be answered.

It is talking about meditation.

To sit silently until your mind is cleared of the chatter, wait until you connect to the energies of the other side.

Jesus spent more time away from people with God in silence having a soul to soul connection instead of blabbering time away.

BACK IN THE THIRD CENTURY

I got the following story from a great book I read a long time ago.

I don't remember the title of the book because I scribbled this on a piece of paper and when I saw it after years I just loved it. The story goes:

> Back in the third century AD, the King Ts'ao sent his son, Prince T'ai to the temple to study under the great master Pan Ku. Because Prince T'ai was to succeed his father as King, Pan Ku was to teach the boy the basics of being a good ruler.

When the prince arrived at the temple, the master sent him alone to the Ming-Li Forest. After one year, the prince was to return to the temple to describe the sound of the forest.

When Prince T'ai returned, Pan Ku asked the boy to describe all that he could hear. "Master," replied the prince, "I could hear the cuckoos sing, the leaves rustle, the hummingbirds hum, the crickets chirp, the grass blow, the bees buzz and the wind whisper and holler."

When the prince had finished, the master told him to go back to the forest to listen to what more he could hear.

The prince was puzzled by the master's request.

Had he not discerned every sound already'?

For days and nights on end the young prince sat alone in the forest listening. But he heard no sounds other than those he had already heard.

Then one morning, as the prince sat silently beneath the trees, he started to discern sounds unlike those he had ever heard before.

The more acutely he listened, the clearer the sounds became. The feeling of enlightenment enveloped the boy. These might be the sounds the master wished me to discern, he reflected.

When Prince T'ai returned to the temple, the master asked him what more he had heard. "Master," responded the prince reverently, "when I listened more closely, I could hear the unheard — the sounds of flowers opening, the sound of the sun warning the earth, and the sound of the grass drinking the morning dew."

The master nodded approvingly: "To hear the unheard," remarked Pan Ku, is a necessary discipline…"

I am talking about developing the discipline of silence until you hear the unheard.

NOISE POLLUTION

One of the greatest obstacles of growth towards your higher self is the fact that we are surrounded by so much noise. Air pollution and water pollution can only hurt the body.

Noise pollution hurts the soul. Have you ever heard these words, 'It's too quiet over here? Can somebody put something on, TV, radio, CD, DVD, anything'!

I have seen people voluntarily drown themselves with noise, creating a silence-less atmosphere almost at will. When they Wake up in the morning they put on the radio or Good Morning South Africa.

They get into their car, and it's already tuned on to their favourite radio station. At work there is enough noise anyway. When they get back home, they get home to a television screen that is already on.

On the weekends they spend their hours between the telly, the radio, the house fly, the bee, the roach and the mosquito. No time to sit alone quietly; no time to reflect upon their life, no time to meditate.

BEING PLUGGED IN

Once you begin to spend moments in silence, about thirty minutes twice a day or more you will begin to realise that behind the apparent separateness that makes the universe, there is perfect unity — that the entire universe is a unified field.

You will begin to realise that you are one with everything else and everybody else. You will also begin to experience this unity in your life in the form of synchronicity.

The term synchronicity was first used by Carl Jung. Jung referred to synchronicity as meaningful coincidence, as when one dreams or thinks of a person and shortly thereafter the person appears or one fantasizes about an event and the event occurs.

For synchronicity to take place two events occur independent of each other, then at some point an individual experiences them together, and in combination they have meaning to that person. It is synchronicity that launches your life onto a magical world. Old African religions seemed to have taught this truth even before the advent of western religions because there is a Sotho adage that goes '*Wa gopola tshukudu namele setlhare*', meaning if you happen to think of a rhino, climb a tree or hide.

This means that your thoughts are not random but connected to the universe or reality.

A couple of years ago while I was in my teens I was invited to go to Swaziland to preach to the royal family. It was during the December holidays. Needless to say I was excited. Meanwhile there was a guy in western Polokwane who was second in charge of a very troubled church organization who decided if there was a person who could help them, it was me.

He wanted me to speak at their year-end convention. There were no cell phones then. He went to Polokwane city and prayed to God he would meet me. I was a student and we rarely went to town.

The day before he went to town I was told that the King had postponed my speaking engagement because of some things had come up. I was disappointed.

The morning of the following day the folks (my friends who lived with me in my double-room at varsity) discovered there was no food and we were all broke. The only thing of value we had was a gold ring given to me by an admirer. I had no choice but to sell the ring or we would starve.

I had to go to town to a jewellery merchant to sell my dear ring.

Just as I came out of the shop I met this gentleman and he told me his story. To cut a long story short I went to *Bochum* instead of Swaziland. But there something strange happened.

A man came and listened to me and saw hopelessly sick people get healed. He left to look for his son who was a lunatic. He found him and brought him to the venue but we had already left.

He asked for the spot where I prayed for people and they showed him. He told his son to go and stand there. The young man was instantly cured of his mental condition. I got this story two months later from the man who had hosted us. What faith?

The universe is so coherent and so much in communication with itself that if you practice meditation and cultivate a life of silence you will be amazed how mystical you really are. I am very sure that my little Swaziland and Bochum story is a small matter compared to what you can tell.

Apart from the benefits of being *plugged in* and having access to strength and information that is not available on the common plane, the practice of silence is able to endow upon you the science, arts, crafts and abilities of the gods.

In silence you can learn manifestation. You can truly become a god and not only create your own world but many other worlds too.

EXERCISING YOUR 'GODNESS'

Sad thing about human beings is they will call themselves children of God, sons of God, etc, but live like mere humans even mammals and not even attempt to stretch forth their divine organs to create miracles.

Let me share with you some of the things that you can exercise that can shift you from human being to divine being. I am not claiming expertise here, however my promise to you at the beginning of this book was simply to wage war against stupidity.

ONE: Mantric Meditation

In the book of Joshua, after the death of Moses, God is said to have told Joshua to meditate on the laws of Moses. "This book of the law shalt not depart from thy mouth but thou shalt meditate therein day and night, for then thou shalt make thy way prosperous and then thou shalt have good success."

This is what most Christians call meditation. It's actually mantric meditation. You take a powerful statement whether from scripture or anywhere and repeat it in your head like a mantra. Best part to do this is before you sleep or just after you wake up.

The more you repeat the statement the more it grows in your system. It can move from just a statement to a belief and then to a knowing. Once it becomes a knowing it will rock your world.

My favourite statement in the past few years was, 'every day in every way I am getting better and better'. I have often inter-changed better for anything from richer to stronger.

TWO: Visualisation and Imagination

Visualization is a powerful tool for creating new worlds, new things. You've got to see it with the eye of your mind or soul to bring it to earth.

Things invisible are creators of the visible.

Some of your silent moments must be used to project with the inner eye how you would like your world to be and what kind of furniture and personnel you want in your life.

Do not be afraid to raise your levels. Just like in a dream where you are not limited by your surroundings refuse the limits in your visualization and they will disappear.

Visualization is the ability to see with your eyes closed. It is not a coincidence that Christ's most popular miracle was the opening of blind eyes. To see or not to see, that is the answer to the question , 'To be or not to be?'

One of my favourite poets is William Blake. He puts everything I was trying to express in one beautiful poem:

> *To see a world in a Grain of Sand*
> *And a Heaven in a Wildflower,*
> *Hold infinity in the palm of your hand,*
> *And eternity in an hour*

Another word that expresses what I am trying to say here is the word 'IMAGINE' - the very important word from Chapter 9. Imagination is the faculty of the gods and I repeat, "You can fly on the wings of your imagination."

What if I told you that God imagined you, and that you might be falling short of his imaginings? What if I told you that Nelson Mandela imagined the new South Africa in his jail cell and that somebody many years ago imagined the cityscape of Pretoria or Tshwane as you see it today and into the future?

What if I told you that almost everything that you see between Pretoria and Johannesburg is some other people's imaginations manifest?

My question to you then — where are the manifestations of your own imaginations'?

Once again, William Blake:

What if you slept?
And what if in your sleep you dreamed
And what if in your dream you went to heaven

And there plucked a strange and beautiful flower
And what when you awoke
You held the flower in your hand.

My dearly departed Siza was very good with entering this state of mind. More than once when we had lost something, she would tap into this realm.

I remember the other time I had misplaced my car keys.

We looked for them for two days and for those days we had to settle for sharing a car. The next night she dreamt and in her dream she saw the keys. She woke up like a sleep walker because she was still asleep and went where she was seeing the keys.

She came back to bed and put them on the bed stand.

In the morning she told me she dreamt the keys and she dreamt going for them and putting them next to the bed. When we looked, to our delight, there they were.

Is it possible to go into the world of dreams and come back with everything that you dreamed manifest in this physical world.

I say it is. I also say it is the faculty of the gods.

Christ said: "Even the least amongst you shall do these things that I do, even greater things..."

The French philosopher and scientist Blaise Pascal said, "All man's miseries derive from not being able to sit quietly in a room, alone".

Depart not from the womb of silence. What gave birth to the miracle that you are will complete it. It is stupid to live your life among the madding crowds.

Thomas Hardy wrote a book and entitled it, 'Far from the Madding Crowds.'

If you want to become a fulfilled Grown-up and fulfill your heroic mission you must live your life, gregarious and sociable as you can be, but still far from the madding crowd. I will retire William Blake and close this chapter with one of my own:

THE WOMB OF SILENCE

I hopped at the border gates of reason
Knocked at the gates of insanity
Trying, plying the doors of unreason
And I found myself at a place called nowhere
I found nowhere preferred to somewhere, anywhere

Cause somewhere brought me where I was
And I loathed the somewhere I inhabited
I know now that genius and insanity are twin sisters
Only raised by different mothers
I stumbled at the feet of wisdom

Yet kissed my lips the grounds of folly
I inquired as in a séance at the courts of sages
And the voices of ages were garbed with the robes of silence
A silence whose loudness so was deafening
And now been deafened I tried, plying the doors of sound

And there was nothing but silence and a silence devoid of any voice
And ah! In silence there I found all the treasures of life
In silence I found reason and sanity

In silence I found wisdom and insanity
In silence I found the womb of creation
I dwelt myself within the walls of her darkness
And there [grew myself the hands of the gods and the wings of angels

There wisdom and knowing replaced reason and folly
For them two, though not twins, nor brothers,
Do drink at the same fount of silence

People go to retreats on mountains to get mental cleansing. Some fast and stay away from food trying to find themselves or their God.

A couple of hungry days later they wake up to the realization that God was never in their stomachs in the first place.

Only the mind is the meeting or contact point between the world of the spirit and the physical world, and it is in cleansing the mind that one can cross over from wherever you are to 'THERE'

. . . to spirit.

"When thinking thoughts are thought, the world around you conspires to create in form your most persistent thoughts."
 - *Vukani Nxumalo*

About

The Author: Moss Mashamaite

MOSS MASHAMAITE is a businessman, a writer and motivational speaker. Some people have dubbed him the social critique or political commentator. What you'll find though is that he is more of a poet, a novelist and often a humorist and satirist.

He is renowned for his hilarious, poignant and provocative style in speech as well as the written word. He's got a truly mighty presentation, one that you will find is irresistible to ignore.

His books in particular are simply not the kind you want to put down because he writes the kind of books even people who do not like books find it hard not to read. A literary artist, an educator and a powerful motivator that's who he is - Moss Mashamaite.

Moss is a graduate of the University of Limpopo where the influence of his ideas was greatly felt by all the came into contact with him. He holds a qualification as an Educator and Degree in Biblical Studies and History. After successfully completing his degrees he went on to further study Engineering with Harcourt College and later earned his PhD in International Trade at Columbus University.

At the time of writing this thought provoking book, he had enthralled more than 100 000 audiences filling speaking engagements for organizations such as, The African National Congress, Uganda Authors' Forum; Metropolitan Life; Pick and Pay; Victory Fellowship, Road Accident Fund; Proudly South African; Felicia Mabuza Suttle Show; Department of Minerals and Energy; Department of Education; Eskom; Nu-Payment Solutions, West Rand Mall Business Owner's Association; Higher Dimensions, and many others.

His other books include but not limited to:

» Ten Stupid Things Grown-Ups Say And Do, It's Official There Is No Cure For Stupidity

» Ten Stupid Things Young People Say And Do, It's Official There Is No Cure For Stupidity

» Ten Stupid Things Married Men Say And Do, It's Official There Is No Cure For Stupidity

Other Stupid Books

...BECAUSE, IT'S OFFICIAL THERE IS NO CURE FOR STUPIDITY

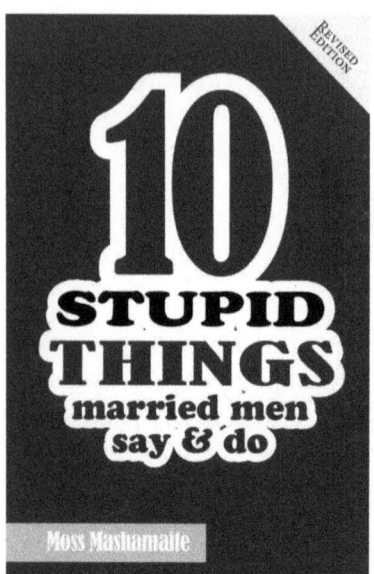
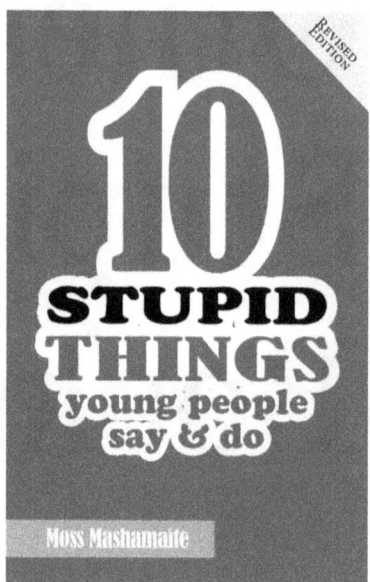
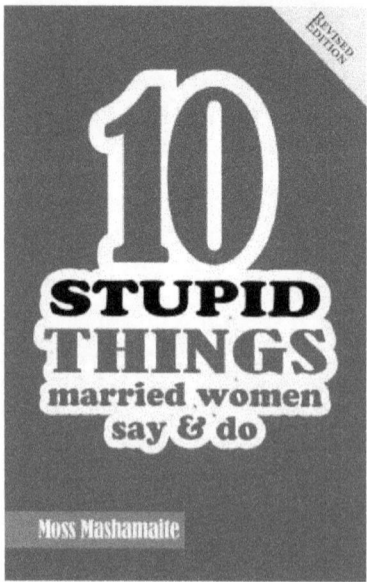

www.ingramcontent.com/pod-product-compliance
Lightning Source LLC
Chambersburg PA
CBHW031258110426
42743CB00040B/730